Fleece Hat Friends

Fleece Hat Friends

25+ easy-to-sew projects

Mary Rasch

LARK CRAFTS

Asheville

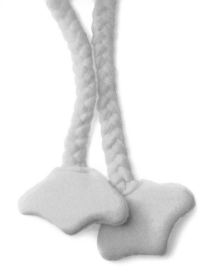

Editor: **Thom O'Hearn**
Art Director: **Megan Kirby**
Designer: **Raquel Joya**
Photographer: **S. Stills**
Illustrations: **Mary Rasch**
Templates: **Orrin Lundgren**
Cover Designer: **Raquel Joya**

An Imprint of Sterling Publishing
387 Park Avenue South
New York, NY 10016

ISBN 978-1-4547-0354-9

Rasch, Mary.
  Fleece hat friends : 25+ easy-to-sew projects / Mary Rasch.
      p. cm.
  Includes bibliographical references and index.
  ISBN 978-1-4547-0354-9 (alk. paper)
1. Machine sewing. 2. Fleece (Textile) 3. Hats. I. Title. II. Title: Twenty-five
plus easy-to-sew projects. III. Title: 25+ easy-to-sew projects.
  TT713.R37 2012
  677'.02864--dc23

2011047739

Distributed in Canada by Sterling Publishing
c/o Canadian Manda Group, 165 Dufferin Street
Toronto, Ontario, Canada M6K 3H6
Distributed in the United Kingdom by GMC Distribution Services
Castle Place, 166 High Street, Lewes, East Sussex, England BN7 1XU
Distributed in Australia by Capricorn Link (Australia) Pty. Ltd.
P.O. Box 704, Windsor, NSW 2756, Australia

For information about custom editions, special sales, and premium and
corporate purchases, please contact Sterling Special Sales at 800-805-5489
or specialsales@sterlingpublishing.com.

Email academic@larkbooks.com for information about desk and examination
copies. The complete policy can be found at larkcrafts.com.

Every effort has been made to ensure that all the information in this book is
accurate. However, due to differing conditions, tools, and individual skills, the
publisher cannot be responsible for any injuries, losses, and other damages
that may result from the use of the information in this book.

Manufactured in China

2 4 6 8 10 9 7 5 3

larkcrafts.com

Contents

6   Basics

20 Projects

20   Feeling Batty

24   Bucktoothed Beaver

28   All a Buzz

32   Beautiful Butterfly

36   Curious Cat

40   Friendly Dinosaur

44   Dinosaur Bag

48   Tall Giraffe

52   Giraffe Scarf

56   Gone Fishing

60   Happy as a Hippo

64   Little Ladybug

68   Lion Around

72   Tails

76   Under the Sea

80   Monkeying Around

84   Monkey Sweatshirt

88   Monster Mash

92   Mouse in the House

96   A Real Hoot

100 Playful Panda

104 Waddling Penguin

108 That's Some Pig

112 Peppy Puppy

116 Floppy-Eared Rabbit

120 Ruler of the Roost

124 Spinning Spider

128 Tame Tiger

132 About the Author

132 Index

Basics

Tools and Materials

Fleece

Where else would I start in a book like this one? Besides being soft, warm, easy to wash, and comfortable to wear, fleece is also a wonderful material to sew with. Since it is quite forgiving, your stitches will sink into the thickness of the fabric as you hum along. But pins will too, so be careful!

Fleece is most commonly sold by the bolt, but it also can also be found in 9 x 12-inch (22.9 x 30.5 cm) sheets. Careful consideration has been made throughout each pattern in this book to guarantee that you can make these hats using either form of fleece, although, if you are like me, you have many fleece remnants in your stash waiting to be used as well. When picking out your fabric, choose a high-quality fleece so there is no need to prewash. Higher grades also ensure your bright, bold colors will not run onto each other in the washing machine.

Fleece comes in two types: regular-grade fleece and anti-pill fleece. Although either type can be used for these projects, you will obviously get the benefit of no pilling from the fabric that has been treated. You will notice that the texture of the anti-pill fleece is nubbier than the untreated fleece.

Although it is sometimes hard to tell, fleece does have a right side and a wrong side. You can tell by tugging along either selvage edge; it will turn upward to the right side of the fabric. If you are unsure which edge is a selvage edge, it is the edge that doesn't stretch as easily. It is always helpful to identify the wrong side by marking your pieces with chalk or marking pencils.

Feel free to take liberties when picking out the colors of your fleece. The suggested colors in each project may not be available, and that is okay. There is no rule that a fish has to be orange. It can be red, green, blue, yellow, brown, or periwinkle. Have fun customizing these hats to your taste!

One last note: Fleece can be washed and dried and it usually holds up very nicely. However, since there are so many hand-sewn embellishments on these hats, I would suggest washing them by hand and hanging them to dry. If a washing machine and dryer are necessary, I would definitely place the hat in a laundry bag to protect the embellishments from agitation.

Pins

As mentioned previously, fleece is thick, which can lead to the temporary loss of a pin. Using long pins with colored-bead heads will help you keep track of them. Always remember to place your pins at a 90° angle to the seam you are going to sew. It is best to remove your pins as your machine approaches them. The needle can often jump the pin, but sometimes it may strike it, which can dull your needle or even break it.

Sewing Needles, Thread, and Embroidery Floss

I recommend a basic sewing needle for all the projects. Most projects work well with a single strand of thread doubled up, and a few will also call for three strands of embroidery floss. Make sure to have needles on hand that can handle the various threads and flosses (and even fishing line) you are using.

I would suggest that you always use a good-quality thread, such as 100 percent polyester. Also, while fleece hides most of your stitching, I've found it is best to use a color that matches or complements the color of the fleece you are working on.

Beads

Don't be frightened; you are not going to be instructed to create intricate beadwork to obtain the glistening look of a wet beaver's tail (although you can if you want!). However, if you are going to make surprised eyes, sleepy eyes, or relaxed eyes, the pattern calls for two beads for the center of the eyes. While picking out your beads, look for ones that are small, black, round, and that have holes all the way through. With tension from the thread, the bead will sink into the white fleece eyeball and hide the holes.

Scissors, Rotary Cutters, Grids, and Mats

You can cut fleece using either sharp scissors or a rotary cutter. Scissors work best for cutting curves or intricate details, while rotary cutters are very useful for accuracy when cutting straight lines. Since fleece can be bulky, make sure to have a 45 mm or 60 mm blade on your rotary cutter if you're using one. This will provide more cutting depth through multiple layers of fleece. If you are using a thick fleece, you may want to cut just one layer at a time.

A self-healing mat is suggested to extend the life of your rotary blade and to protect the surface of your cutting area.

A grid will help to keep your cuts straight and will aid in measuring. For safety, finger guards can be purchased for your grid—a very good idea!

Sewing Machine

Any sewing machine will do. Just make sure that it is in proper working order. It helps to have a new, sharp needle. Select a needle size that is meant for the weight of your fleece—generally for fleece it will be size 14. Your local fabric store can help you identify the weight of your fabric or fleece, and the appropriate needle size.

Polyester Fiberfill

You will be stuffing many of the facial features of your hat with fiberfill. You can choose polyester fiberfill—a synthetic material that works well to give dimension to your project. It is lightweight and keeps its shape when washed. Another option, if you prefer to be environmentally friendly, is Ingeo fiberfill. It works the same as polyester fiberfill but it is made from 100 percent annually renewable resources.

Tracing Paper, Tissue Paper, or Interfacing

In order to keep the patterns in this book intact and ready for future hats (believe me, they are addicting, and you won't be able to stop at just one!), copy the patterns using tracing paper, a light-color tissue paper, or interfacing. Interfacing is fairly new to me for tracing patterns, but I like that it does not slip when placed on your fabric, and it's relatively inexpensive. Note that you will need to need to enlarge some patterns, in which case you can use the local copy shop or your own scanner/printer.

Washable Fabric Glue

There are no secrets or suggestions for this supply; just go to your craft or fabric store and pick your favorite washable fabric glue.

Pipe Cleaners

Many of the critters in this book have either antennas or tails that call for a pipe cleaner to help with structure. Purchase standard-sized pipe cleaners in any color; they will be covered up by fleece.

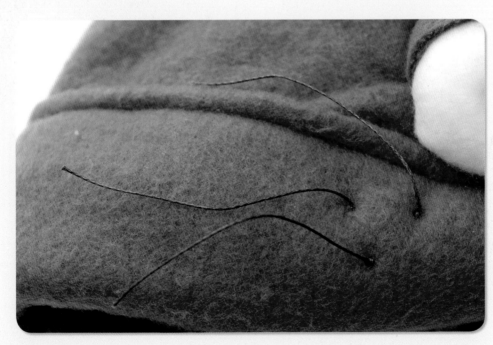

Basic Sewing Tool Kit

The following items are going to be used the most when making the projects in this book so keep them on hand!

- Chalk or washable fabric marking pen
- Grid
- Long straight pins with bead heads
- Mat
- Rotary cutter
- Scissors
- Sewing machine
- Sewing needles
- Tape measure or ruler
- Thread

Straws

Yes, straws! It may seem like an unusual material for this list, but projects like the Spinning Spider hat (page 124) need straws to give its legs structure. A box of standard bendable straws of any color will do.

Black Fishing Line

I found that black fishing line worked well for the animals' whiskers since it knots and is pliable (plus it won't poke someone's eye out). Sporting goods stores often sell black fishing line by the yard—so go for the thickest they carry.

How to Make the Basic Hat

Before you begin, select the critter you are going to make and check what colors of fleece the top of the hat and the brim require. You will need ¼ yard (22.9 cm) of fleece in each of these colors, which will be enough for the basic hat of any size listed below, as long as your fleece is 60 inches (1.5 m) wide. If you're using 9 x 12-inch (22.9 x 30.5 cm) sheets of fleece, the materials list for each hat will tell you how much of each color you will need.

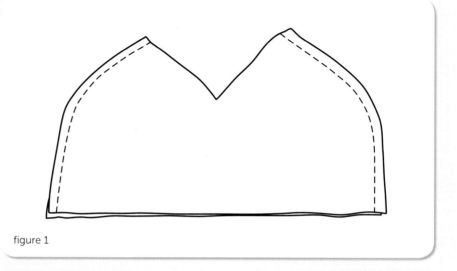

figure 1

Instructions

1 Copy the templates for the Basic Hat Top (page 17) and Basic Hat Brim (page 16) in your desired size on tissue paper, tracing paper, or interfacing. Note that if you're using 9 x 12-inch (22.9 x 30.5 cm) fleece sheets, you will need to copy the Fleece Sheets Basic Hat Brim on page 18. Cut them out.

2 Using the suggested color for the top of your hat, pin the Basic Hat Top template onto your fleece (going with the stretch of the fabric) and cut it out. Repeat this step to produce two Basic Hat Top pieces total.

3 With right sides together, sew from the bottom edge up to the point on both edges of the hat **(figure 1)**.

4 Refold the hat with right sides together to create an arc. Make sure to pin the very top where the seams meet so they align perfectly, and then sew along the arc **(figure 2)**.

5 If you are using fleece off the bolt, use the suggested color for the brim of your hat, and fold one selvage edge toward the other selvage edge allowing enough doubled-up material for the pattern to be placed. Pin the Basic Hat Brim template with its left side on the fold of the fabric, as indicated on the pattern, going with the stretch. Once cut, fold this piece so the right sides are together and sew the short ends together.

Size	Head Circumference	Generally Fits
Extra Small (XS)	20 Inches (50.8 cm)	Child
Small (S)	21 Inches (53.3 cm)	Youth
Medium (M)	22 Inches (55.9 cm)	Women
Large (L)	23 Inches (58.4 cm)	Men

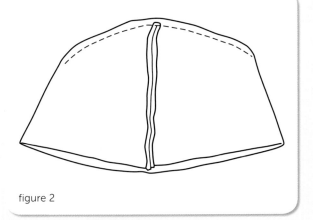

figure 2

If you're using 9 x 12-inch (22.9 x 30.5 cm) sheets of fleece, use the suggested color for the brim of your hat. Pin the template for the Fleece Sheets Basic Hat Brim in place and cut four pieces. Once cut, place two pieces together so the right sides are facing and sew along one short end. Repeat for the remaining two pieces. Place both newly sewn pieces with right sides together and sew both short ends together. Trim all edges sewn up to this point.

6 With the wrong side facing out on both pieces, tuck the hat top into the brim and align the bottom edges (the wrong side of the hat should be facing the right side of the brim). Pin around the straight edge and sew around the edge (**figure 3**).

Suggestion: If you do not want a seam coming down between the eyes in the front of the hat, position the brim's seam halfway between the two seams that come all the way down to the bottom edge on the top of the hat.

7 Unfold the hat so the top has its right side facing out and the brim is hanging below with the wrong side facing out. Fold the bottom of the hat up to the seam just sewn and fold it again to create the brim. Adjust as necessary. Depending on the person wearing the hat, you may need less of a brim. In that case, unfold the cuff, trim, and refold it.

Note: Since wings, antenna, or fins may be tucked into the brim, we will leave the top edge loose for now. It will be sewn in place in the instructions for your critter.

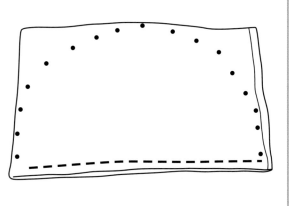

figure 3

A Note About Seams

Most seams are ¼ inch (6 mm) throughout the book unless otherwise noted. Before you start your project, double-check where the ¼-inch (6 mm) mark is on your sewing machine. It will make a difference in the size of your hat if you sway from this seam allowance.

You'll see that the individual hat templates are marked with lines where I recommend machine stitching and hand stitching the pieces. Note that for most attachments (ears, horns, spots, noses, and eyes) you can use whatever stitch you like. I tend to go with a ladder stitch—if the stitch shows, it will look nice.

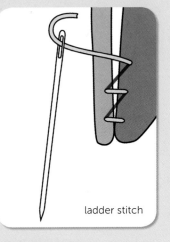

ladder stitch

11

Earflaps, Braids, and Tassels

It is up to you whether or not you want to add earflaps, braids, and tassels. Many projects are shown with them—some even have decorative paws or claws attached! They are a simple addition, so you can decide anytime during your project whether or not you want them. However, if you are adding them and the example pictured does not have them, plan on adding an extra ¼ yard (22.9 cm) of material or three 9 x 12-inch (22.9 x 30.5 cm) sheets to your materials list.

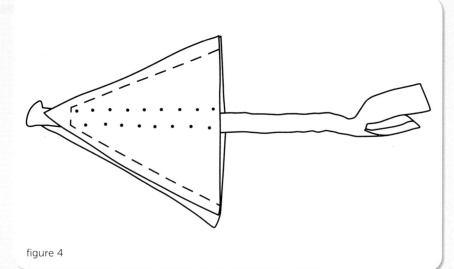

figure 4

1 Start by cutting six 1-inch-wide (2.5 cm) strips from your fleece. The length of these strips, and therefore the braids, depends on personal preference. If you are unsure what length would be appropriate and would like a suggestion for the different sizes, make 6-inch (15.2 cm) braids for Extra-Small hats, 9-inch (22.9 cm) braids for Small hats, and 12-inch (30.5 cm) braids for Medium and Large hats. Note also that almost 1 inch (2.5 cm) of this braid length will be sewn into the earflap.

2 Stack three of these pieces and sew across the top to join them. Attach a safety pin to the top of the three pieces and connect it to something stable that will not snag (such as the rug beneath you, the shoelace on the shoe you are wearing, or even the bottom cuff of your pants). Create a uniform braid from the three strips and knot them at the bottom once you reach your desired length. Make sure to leave 2 inches (5.1 cm) unbraided at the bottom end of your strips for tassels. You can create more "strands" in your tassel by cutting vertically through the middle of each strip. Repeat to make the second braid.

3 Cut four Earflaps using the template in the color indicated in the project instructions. Place two triangles together with right sides facing each other, and sandwich one of your braids inside. Make sure the stitched end is sticking out at the point of the triangle so it is sewn into the seam. Pin these pieces together and sew along the markings on the pattern. When you are nearing the point of the triangle, turn and sew across it to the other side of the flap **(figure 4)**.

Your machine will be going through many layers of fleece at this time, so be sure to help it by guiding the pieces through at a steady pace. Once you reach the other side, turn the piece so that you are heading back up the

triangle. Turn the earflap so the right sides face out. Repeat these sewing instructions to create the other earflap.

4 Attach both earflaps by hand sewing them to the inside of the hat along the seam that you made to sew the brim in place. Be sure to center the earflaps along each side of the hat with the best sides of your braids facing outward.

How to Make the Lining (optional)

Although a lining is not necessary, you may want to add one for warmth or for a more finished look. Since this lining adds another layer of fleece or other material of your choice, it will create more bulk, so you may want to select the next size up if you are concerned about too snug a fit. The lining is the very last step to your hat, so come back to these instructions once your critter has been created.

1 In either the main hat color or a coordinating color, cut two pieces using the Basic Hat Top template (page 17).

2 With right sides together, sew from the bottom edge up to the top point on both edges of the hat (see figure 1 on page 10).

3 Refold the hat with right sides together to create an arc. Make sure to pin the very top where the seams meet so they align perfectly (see figure 2 on page 11).

4 Instead of turning this piece right side out, you are going to nest it inside the main hat shell so the wrong sides are together. Fold the bottom edges in until they line up with the seam that connects brim to the top of the hat and pin.

5 Hand sew the lining in place using a thread that's the same color as the fleece. As you sew, do not come through to the outside of the hat with your stitches.

Eyes

On these two pages you'll find instructions for creating five different types of eyes, but feel free to use your imagination to create whatever style you would like. So much expression can be conveyed just through the eyes of your critter.

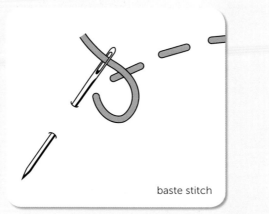

baste stitch

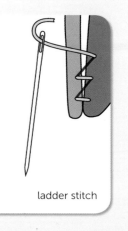

ladder stitch

Tools and Materials

- Basic Sewing Tool Kit
- Scraps of white fleece, approximately 4 inches (10.2 cm) square, or 2 inches (5.1 cm) square if making the mini eyes
- Scraps of fleece for eyelids (optional), approximately 4 inches (10.2 cm) square
- Black beads (I use either 6 or 8 mm)
- Fabric glue

to the front to catch the bead by going through the hole in the center. Repeat until the bead is secure. Go back through the eyeball and pull the thread tight so that the bead sinks slightly into the eye. Repeat for the second eye.

3 Hand sew your eyes to the hat using a ladder stitch. Pull your stitches tight so they hide in the fleece. I like to place the eyes so they are touching in the center!

Surprised Eyes

1 Cut two pieces out of white fleece using the Surprised Eye template (page 19). Loosely baste stitch around the outer edge of this circle and pull loosely to create a pouch. Stuff a small amount of fiberfill in this pouch, cinch it shut, and stitch the opening closed.

2 Place a black bead on the center of the eye. With your needle and thread, come from the back of the eyeball

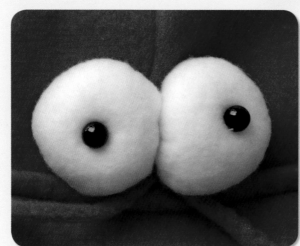

Mini Surprised Eyes

1 Cut two pieces out of white fleece using the Mini Surprised Eye template (page 19).

2 Follow the instructions on this page for Surprised Eyes.

Note: By tilting the eyelids one way or another, you can achieve many different expressions.

3 Hand sew your eyes to the hat using a ladder stitch. Pull your stitches tight so they hide in the fleece.

Sleepy Eyes

Follow the instructions for the Relaxed Eyes on this page using the Sleepy Eyelid template (page 19) instead of the Relaxed Eyelid template.

Beady Eyes

Attach two small black beads directly on the hat. Embroider eyebrows just above the beads if you desire.

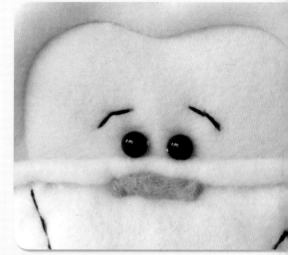

Relaxed Eyes

By adding a simple eyelid, you can give your critter oodles of expressions. To make relaxed eyes, follow step 1 of the Surprised Eyes on the previous page and then proceed with the steps below.

1 Cut two pieces out of your hat's top color using the Relaxed Eyelid template (page 19). Place the straight edge of the fleece so it covers half of the eye. Place some fabric glue at the top of the eyeball before wrapping the eyelid around it (this is to make sure the lid doesn't pop up off the eye over time). Let the glue dry.

2 Baste stitch around the curved edge of the eyelid as marked in the pattern. Pull the thread just as you did to create the eyeball. Stitch the eyelid in place on the back. Secure your bead in place as desired.

Basic Hat Templates

enlarge template by 200%
or use chart

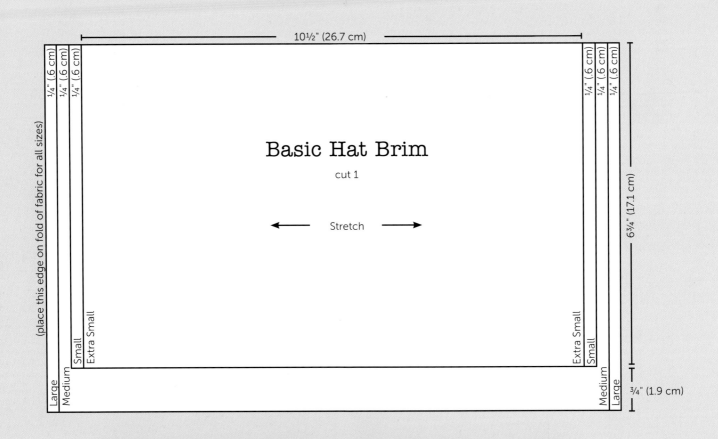

Basic Hat Brim

cut 1

← Stretch →

10½" (26.7 cm)

¼" (.6 cm) ¼" (.6 cm) ¼" (.6 cm)

(place this edge on fold of fabric for all sizes)

Large Medium Small Extra Small

6¾" (17.1 cm)

¾" (1.9 cm)

Size	Length	Width
Extra Small (XS)	6¾ Inches (17.1 cm)	10½ Inches (26.7 cm)
Small (S)	6¾ Inches (17.1 cm)	11 Inches (27.9 cm)
Medium (M)	7½ Inches (19 cm)	11½ Inches (29.2 cm)
Large (L)	7½ Inches (19 cm)	12 Inches (30.5 cm)

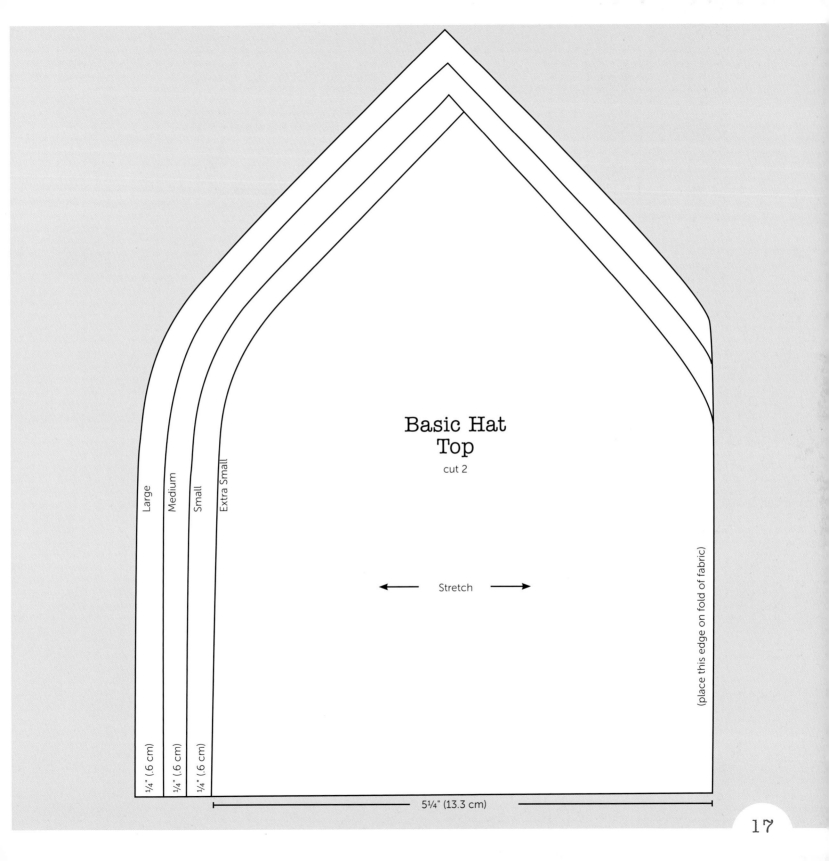

**Basic Hat
Top**

cut 2

Large

Medium

Small

Extra Small

¼" (.6 cm)

¼" (.6 cm)

¼" (.6 cm)

← Stretch →

(place this edge on fold of fabric)

5¼" (13.3 cm)

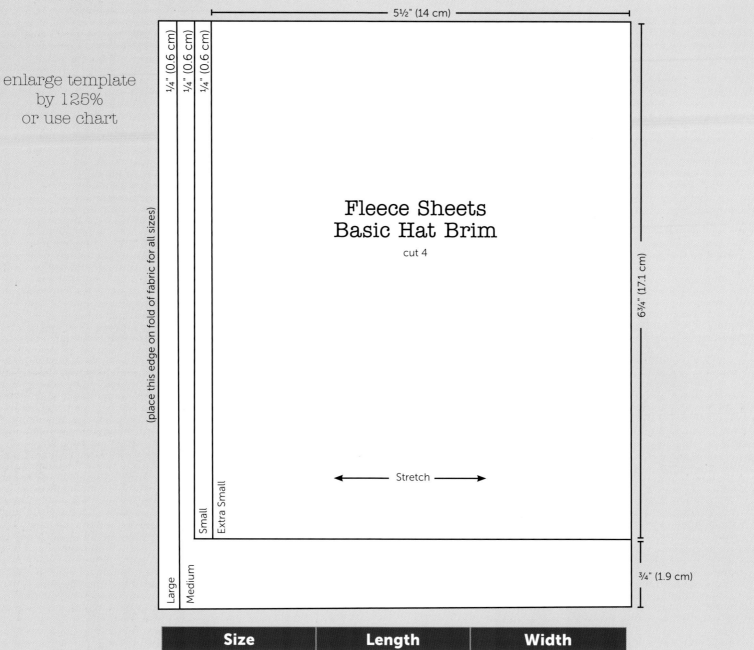

enlarge template by 125% or use chart

5½" (14 cm)

¼" (0.6 cm) ¼" (0.6 cm) ¼" (0.6 cm)

(place this edge on fold of fabric for all sizes)

Large Medium Small Extra Small

Fleece Sheets
Basic Hat Brim

cut 4

⟵ Stretch ⟶

6¾" (17.1 cm)

¾" (1.9 cm)

Size	Length	Width
Extra Small (XS)	6¾ Inches (17.1 cm)	5½ Inches (26.7 cm)
Small (S)	6¾ Inches (17.1 cm)	5¾ Inches (27.9 cm)
Medium (M)	7½ Inches (19 cm)	6 Inches (29.2 cm)
Large (L)	7½ Inches (19 cm)	6¼ Inches (30.5 cm)

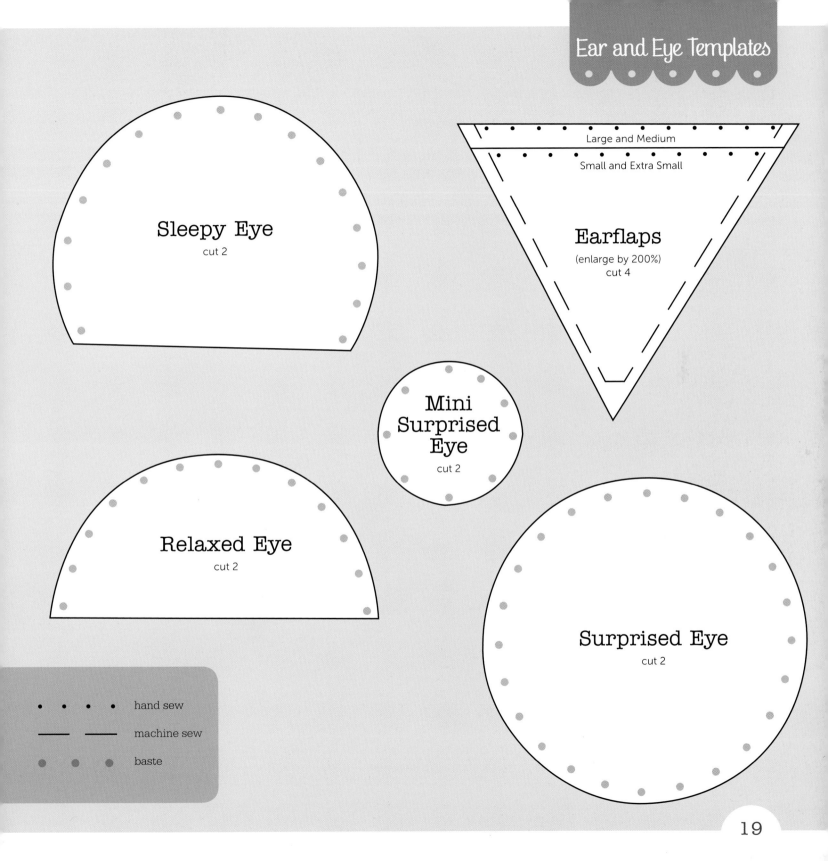

Sleepy Eye
cut 2

Earflaps
(enlarge by 200%)
cut 4

Large and Medium

Small and Extra Small

**Mini
Surprised
Eye**
cut 2

Relaxed Eye
cut 2

Surprised Eye
cut 2

· · · ·   hand sew

——— ——   machine sew

● ● ●   baste

19

Feeling Batty

This is the perfect hat come Halloween!

Tools and Materials

- Basic Sewing Tool Kit (page 9)
- ¼ yard (22.9 cm) of orange fleece (solid or tie-dyed)
- ¼ yard (22.9 cm) of black fleece
- Polyester fiberfill
- Black beads, fleece, polyester fiberfill for eyes

{ If you're using 9 x 12-inch (22.9 x 30.5 cm) sheets of fleece, you will need 6 sheets of orange fleece (solid or tie-dyed) and 3 sheets of black fleece. }

Instructions

1 Using the instructions and templates for the Basic Hat (page 10), create your hat using tie-dyed or solid orange fleece.

2 Topstitch ¼ inch (6 mm) down from the top edge of the brim to secure it in place.

3 Cut four Wing pieces from black fleece using the template, two with the pattern facing up and two with the pattern facing down. Take two of the wings, place them with right sides together, and machine sew along the edge of the wings as marked on your pattern. Turn the wing right side out and machine sew the details as marked on the pattern. Repeat this step for the second wing.

4 Cut two Head pieces from black fleece using the template. Place them with right sides together and machine sew along the edge of the face as marked on your pattern, leaving an opening at the bottom. Turn the face piece right side out and loosely stuff it with fiberfill. Tuck in the unsewn edges at the bottom and hand sew the opening shut.

5 Cut two Ear pieces from black fleece using the template and hand sew the marked edge onto the back of the head, one on each side.

6 Select the type of eyes you would like (Mini Surprised or Beady) from the Basics section (page 14). Attach the eyes on the face and add another black bead near the bottom of the face for the nose.

7 Center the wings on the front of the hat with the open straight edges touching and hand sew them on. Hand sew the head in place on top of the wings, covering the stitching you just completed. As a final step, tack the wings to the hat to keep them from flopping forward.

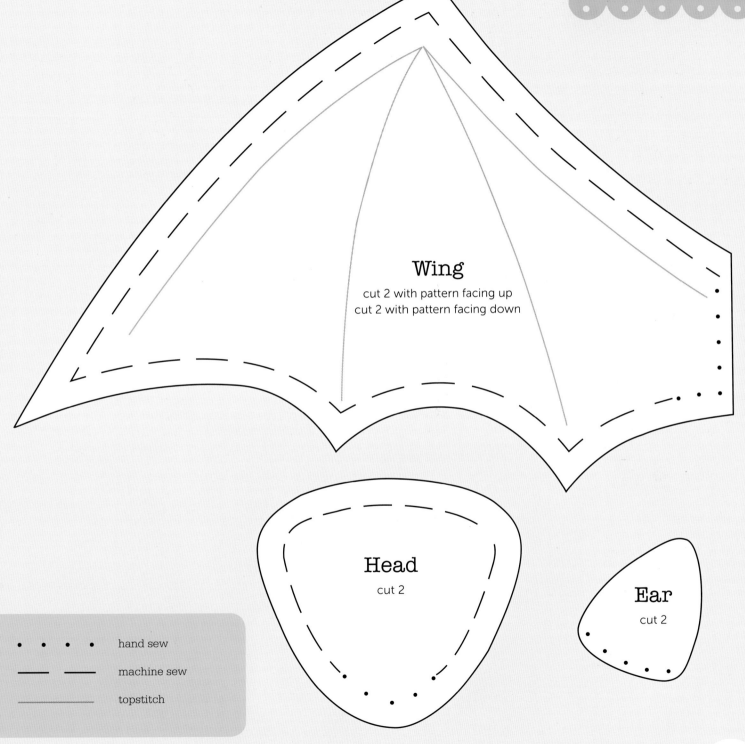

Wing

cut 2 with pattern facing up
cut 2 with pattern facing down

Head

cut 2

Ear

cut 2

· · · · · hand sew

— — — machine sew

———— topstitch

Bucktoothed Beaver

The big, floppy tail steals
the show in this design.

Tools and Materials

- Basic Sewing Tool Kit (page 9)
- ¼ yard (22.9 cm) of dark brown fleece
- ¼ yard (22.9 cm) of light brown fleece
- Scrap of black fleece
- Polyester fiberfill
- Black beads for eyes
- Scrap of off-white fleece

{ If you're using 9 x 12-inch (22.9 x 30.5 cm) sheets of fleece you will need 4 sheets of dark brown fleece, 4 sheets of light brown fleece, 1 sheet or scrap of black fleece, and 1 sheet or scrap of off-white fleece. }

Instructions

1 Using the instructions and templates for the Basic Hat (page 10), create your hat using dark brown fleece for the top and light brown fleece for the brim.

2 Topstitch ¼ inch (6 mm) down from the top edge of the brim to secure it in place.

3 To create a curved lip, find the vertical seam on the brim of the hat and roll the bottom of it up slightly toward the inside of the hat. Stitch it in place.

4 Cut one oval Nose piece out of black fleece using the template. Baste stitch around the outer edge of this oval and pull the thread loosely to create a pouch. Stuff a small amount of fiberfill in this pouch, cinch it shut, and stitch the opening closed. Begin pinching one section of the pouch to create the bottom section of the nose. To create nostril indents, go back and forth pulling tightly with needle and thread between the two dots marked on your pattern. Attach the nose near the top of the vertical seam, but below the seam going around the top of the brim.

5 Select the type of eyes you would like from the Basics section (page 14). Attach the eyes just above the brim on the front of the hat.

6 Cut two Teeth pieces from off-white fleece using the template. With right sides together, sew three sides of the teeth, leaving the top open as marked on your pattern. Turn the teeth right side out and machine sew a line of stitching going up the middle to create two separate teeth. Depending on how much you would like showing, pin the teeth in place, centered under the curved lip, and hand sew them on the inside of the brim.

7 Cut out four Ear pieces from your dark brown fleece using the templates. Place two pieces with right sides together and sew along the curved part of the ear, leaving the straight edge open as marked on your pattern. Repeat for the second ear. Turn both ears so the right sides are facing out. Fold the unfinished edge of the ear in half along the line marked on the pattern. Hand sew the unfinished edge together and pin one ear on each side of the hat. Feel free to take liberties with the positioning of the ears as you hand sew them in place.

8 Cut two Tail pieces out of dark brown fleece using the template. With right sides together, sew along the curved edge, leaving the straight section open as marked on the pattern. Flip the tail so the right sides are facing out and sew along the curved edge once again, this time topstitching ⅝ inch (1.6 cm) from the outer edge.

9 Using the template as your guide, mark the diagonal lines on your tail with pins or chalk. Carefully machine sew along your markings to create the crosshatch pattern. When the grid is complete, attach the tail by hand sewing it on the inside of the back of the brim.

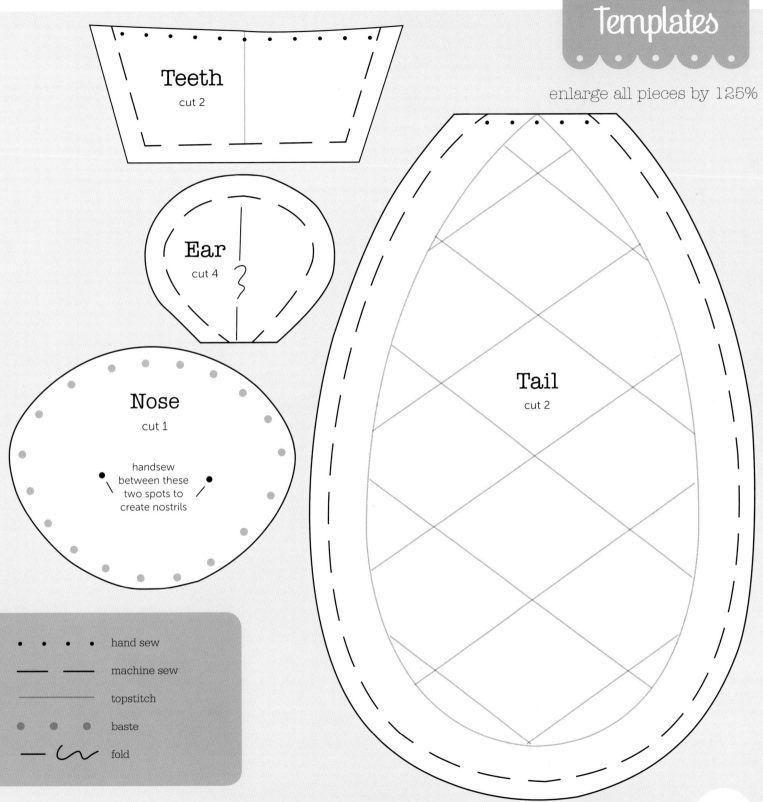

enlarge all pieces by 125%

Teeth
cut 2

Ear
cut 4

Nose
cut 1

handsew between these two spots to create nostrils

Tail
cut 2

- • • • • hand sew
- — — machine sew
- ——— topstitch
- • • • baste
- ∿ fold

All a Buzz

This is one busy bee nobody has to run away from!

Tools and Materials

- Basic Sewing Tool Kit (page 9)
- ¼ yard (22.9 cm) of yellow fleece
- ¼ yard (22.9 cm) of black fleece
- ⅛ yard (11.4 cm) of white fleece
- 1 pipe cleaner
- Two ½ inch (1.3 cm) black or yellow pom-poms
- Black beads, fleece, polyester fiberfill for eyes
- Polyester fiberfill

{ If you're using 9 x 12-inch (22.9 x 30.5 cm) sheets of fleece you will need 2 sheets of yellow fleece, 4 sheets of black fleece, and 1 sheet of white fleece. }

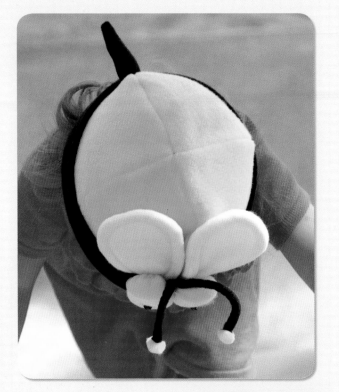

Instructions

1 Using the instructions and template for the Basic Hat (page 10), create your hat using yellow fleece for the top and black fleece for the brim.

2 Cut four Wing pieces from white fleece using the template, two with the pattern facing up and two with the pattern facing down. Place two pieces with right sides together and machine sew around the curved edge of the wing, leaving the straight edge open as marked on your pattern. Turn the wing right side out and sew around the curve, this time topstitching ¼ inch (6 mm) from the edge. Repeat this step for the second wing.

3 On the front of your hat, tuck the bottom ½ inch (1.3 cm) of your wings under the brim. Pin them in place and machine stitch through all layers ¼ inch (6 mm) down from the top edge of the brim to secure the brim and wings in place. Your machine will be going through many layers of fleece when going over the wings, so guide everything forward carefully. After you are done, tack the wings in place to the hat to make sure they stay upright.

4 Next, create the antennas by cutting a pipe cleaner to 8 inches (20.3 cm) in length. Cut one Antenna piece out of black fleece using the template. Wrap the fleece around the pipe cleaner and ladder stitch along all the edges. Sew one pom-pom on each end of the antenna. Form the antenna into a V shape and bend the ends forward slightly. Sew the antenna in place directly above the brim on top of the wings.

5 Select the type of eyes you would like from the Basics section (page 14). Attach the eyes, overlapping the brim, on top of the wings and antenna on the front of the hat.

6 Cut one Stinger piece from black fleece using the template. Fold it according to the pattern so the right sides are together and sew along the marked edge. Turn it right side out and stuff it with fiberfill to help the stinger keep its shape. Pin it right above the brim on the back of the hat and hand sew it in place.

Variation: Just like the Little Ladybug (page 64), this hat is very sweet looking and less cartoonlike if you opt to go without an eye embellishment.

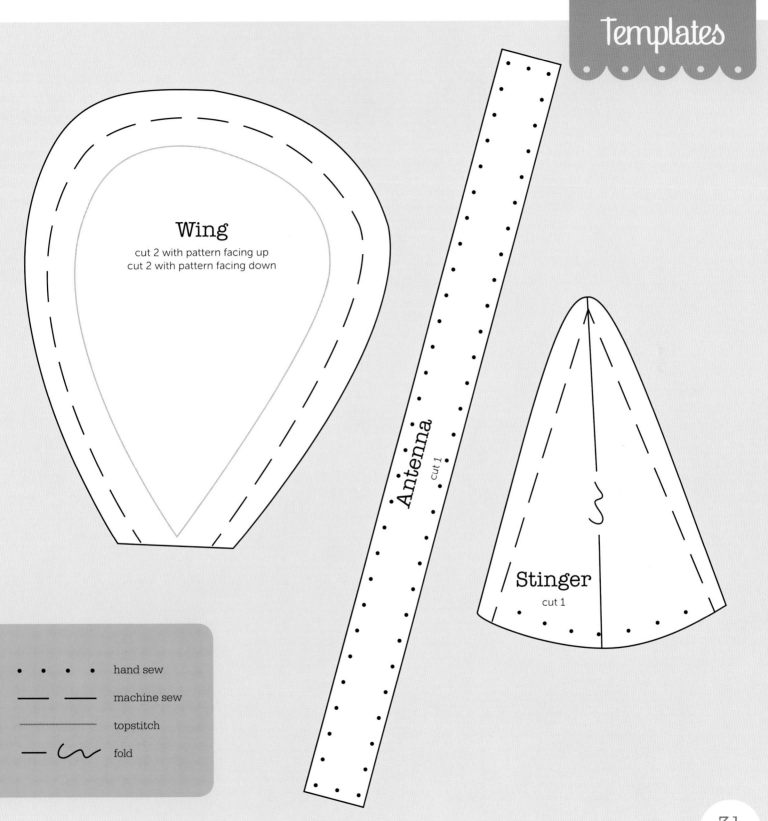

Wing

cut 2 with pattern facing up
cut 2 with pattern facing down

Antenna cut 1

Stinger

cut 1

· · · · · hand sew

——— ——— machine sew

············· topstitch

——— ⌒ fold

Beautiful Butterfly

Get your nets ready. This butterfly makes for a fun springtime hat.

Tools and Materials

- Basic Sewing Tool Kit (page 9)
- ¼ yard (22.9 cm) of black fleece
- ¼ yard (22.9 cm) of tie-dyed fleece
- Scrap of purple fleece
- Polyester fiberfill
- Black beads for eyes
- Black fishing line

{ If you're using 9 x 12-inch (22.9 x 30.5 cm) sheets of fleece you will need 6 sheets of black fleece, 2 sheets of tie-dyed fleece (for wings), and 1 sheet or scrap of purple fleece. }

Instructions

1 Using the instructions and template for the Basic Hat (page 10), create your hat. The hat shown was made from black fleece so that the wing colors would pop. However, feel free to experiment with any color you would like.

2 Topstitch ¼ inch (6 mm) down from the top edge of the brim to secure it in place.

3 Cut four Top Wing pieces from tie-dyed fleece using the template: two with the pattern facing up and two with the pattern facing down. If you are using a patterned fleece, be careful to cut the wings from similar areas of the pattern so they match. Place two of the wings with right sides together and sew around the outer edge of the wing, leaving the straight edge open as marked on your pattern. Turn the wings right side out and machine sew the details as marked on the pattern. Feel free to stuff the wing slightly with fiberfill to give it structure; however, do not overstuff it as butterfly wings are supposed to be flat, not puffy. Repeat this step for the second top wing.

4 Repeat step 3, only this time for the two Bottom Wings of the butterfly.

5 Cut two Body pieces from your purple fleece using the template. With right sides together, sew around the edge, leaving the end of the butterfly open as marked on the pattern. Turn right side out and lightly stuff this tube with fiberfill. Hand sew the open end of the butterfly shut. Thread your needle and make a knot. At the location marked on your pattern, insert the needle from the underside, through the body, then wrap the thread around the body twice, pulling it tightly to create a head. Knot your thread and cut it.

6 On either side of your butterfly body, hand sew both sets of top and bottom wings.

7 Hand sew the butterfly to the hat in any spot you prefer.

8 Select the type of eyes you would like from the Basics section (page 14). Note that the Mini Surprised Eyes and Beady Eyes work best for the small face of the butterfly.

9 Using black fishing line and your needle, create antenna on the head of the butterfly. Insert your needle behind one eye and bring it out behind the other. Trim to your desired length and knot each antenna next to the fleece to keep them in place. Knot them once again at the tips.

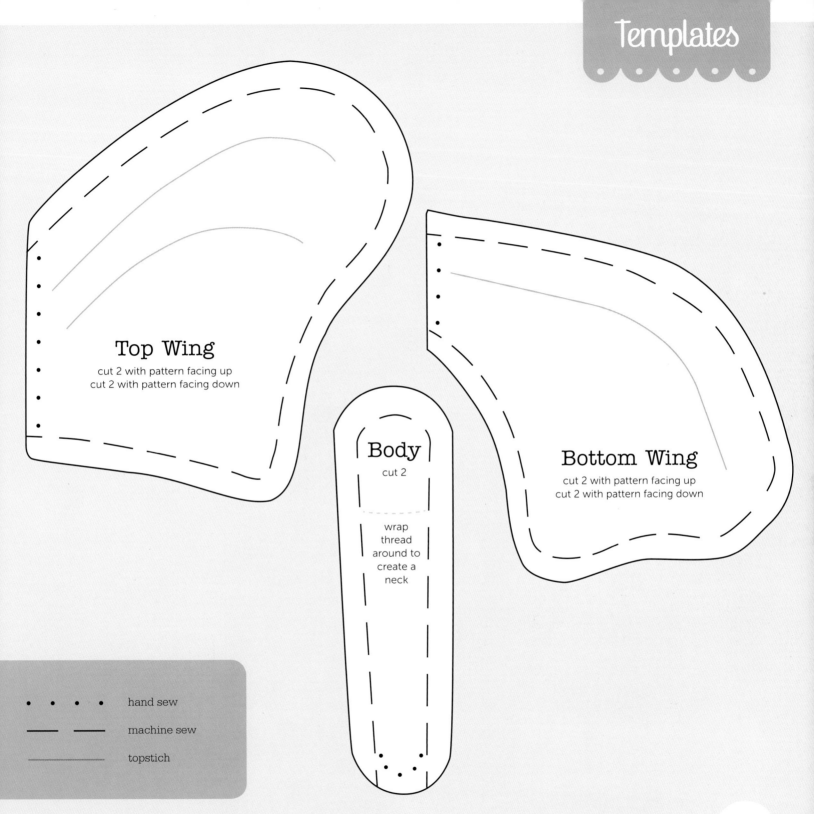

Top Wing

cut 2 with pattern facing up
cut 2 with pattern facing down

Body

cut 2

wrap
thread
around to
create a
neck

Bottom Wing

cut 2 with pattern facing up
cut 2 with pattern facing down

• • • • hand sew

— — — machine sew

———— topstich

35

Curious Cat

The "purr-fect" design for friends of felines.

Tools and Materials

- Basic Sewing Tool Kit (page 9)
- ½ yard (45.7 cm) of purple fleece
- Scrap of pink fleece
- Black beads, fleece, polyester fiberfill for eyes
- Polyester fiberfill
- Black fishing line

If you're using 9 x 12-inch (22.9 x 30.5 cm) sheets of fleece, you will need 9 sheets of purple fleece and 1 sheet or large scrap of pink fleece.

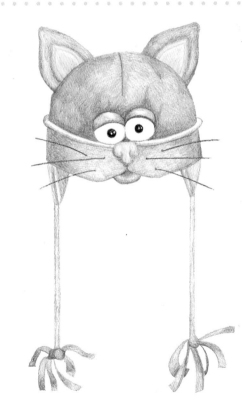

Instructions

1 Using the instructions and templates for the Basic Hat (page 10), create your hat using purple fleece.

2 Topstitch ¼ inch (6 mm) down from the top edge of the brim to secure it in place.

3 To create a curved lip, find the vertical seam on the brim of the hat and roll the bottom half of it up toward the inside of the hat. Stitch it in place.

4 Cut two Mouth pieces from purple fleece using the template. Sew around the curved edge, leaving the straight edge open as marked on your pattern. Flip the mouth right side out and guide your finger along the inside of the seam to smooth out any waviness. Then sew the mouth piece in place on the inside of the brim, making sure it is down far enough to be visible.

5 Cut four Outer Ear pieces from purple fleece and two Inner Ear pieces out of pink fleece using the templates. Lining up the straight edges and centering the pink fleece, machine sew each Inner Ear on the right side of an Outer Ear piece. These are now the front of the ears, and the pieces without the pink fleece are the backs.

6 Place one back of the ear and one front of the ear with right sides together. Sew along the two curved edges, leaving the straight edge open as marked on your pattern. Turn the ear right side out and guide your finger along the inside of the seam to smooth it out. Repeat this step for the second ear. Hand sew the ears on either side of the hat.

7 Select the type of eyes you would like from the Basics section (page 14). Attach the eyes just above the brim on the front of the hat.

8 Cut one Nose piece from pink fleece using the template. Baste stitch around the outer edge and pull the

thread to create a pouch. Stuff a small amount of fiberfill in this pouch, cinch it shut, and sew the opening closed. To create nostrils, go back and forth pulling tightly with needle and thread between the two dots marked on your pattern. Attach the nose near the top of the vertical seam, and let the nose overlap the top edge of the brim.

9 Thread a needle with black fishing line and make a knot at the end of the line. At the desired location for a whisker on the brim, pull the needle from the inside of the hat and exit out the front. Make a knot next to the fleece to keep the whisker in place and trim it to about 3 inches (7.6 cm) in length. Repeat this step so that you have three whiskers on each cheek.

10 Refer to Earflaps, Braids, and Tassels instructions in the Basics section (page 12) to add these features.

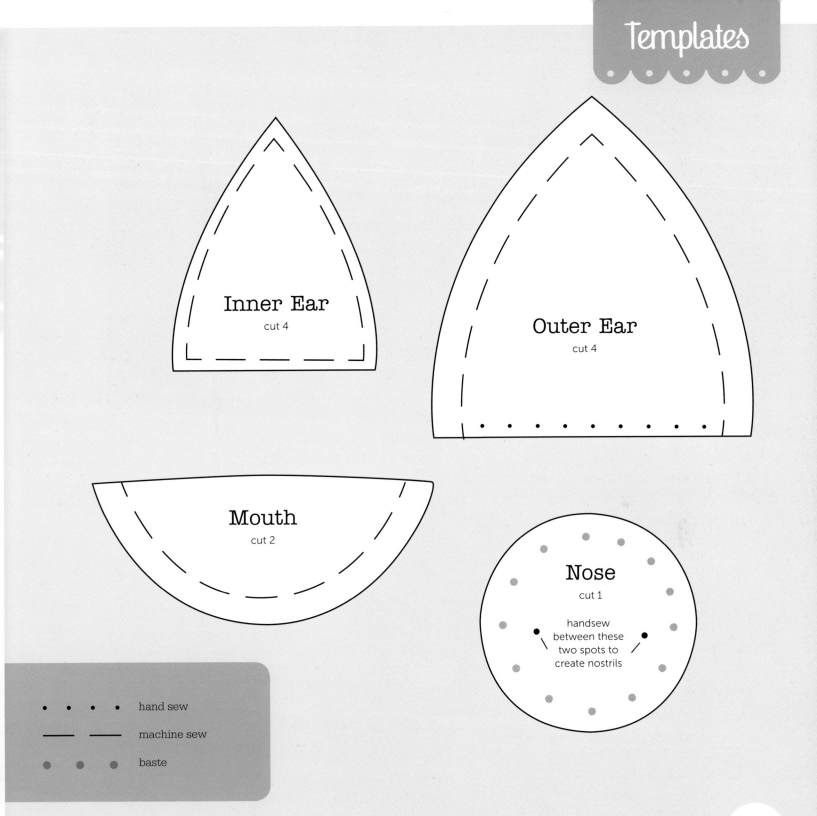

Inner Ear
cut 4

Outer Ear
cut 4

Mouth
cut 2

Nose
cut 1

handsew
between these
two spots to
create nostrils

• • • • hand sew

——— machine sew

● ● ● baste

Friendly Dinosaur

Is your kiddo interested in exploring the Jurassic period?

Tools and Materials

- Basic Sewing Tool Kit (page 9)
- ¼ yard (22.9 cm) of green fleece (solid or tie-dyed)
- ⅛ yard (11.4 cm) of brown fleece
- Scrap of white fleece
- Polyester fiberfill
- Black beads, fleece, polyester fiberfill for eyes (optional)

{ If you're using 9 x 12-inch (22.9 x 30.5 cm) sheets of fleece you will need 6 sheets of green fleece (solid or tie-dyed), 2 sheets of brown fleece, and 1 sheet or scrap of white fleece. }

Instructions

1 Using the instructions and templates for the Basic Hat (page 10), create your hat using tie-dyed or solid green fleece. The hat shown here was made from tie-dyed fleece, which creates a fun texture for your dinosaur.

2 Topstitch ¼ inch (6 mm) down from the top edge of the brim to secure it in place.

3 Cut eight Spike pieces out of brown fleece using the template. With right sides together, machine sew along the curved edges of the spike, leaving the straight edge open. Turn the spike right side out and topstitch ⅝ inch (1.6 cm) from the outer edge, following the markings on the pattern. Repeat this step three more times to create four spikes total.

4 Stuff the spikes with fiberfill and hand sew them on, starting the first spike at the back of the hat on the bottom of the brim. Continue attaching each spike, following the seam running from front to back.

5 Select the type of eyes you would like from the Basics section (page 14). Hand sew the eyes on the brim on the front of the hat.

6 Cut two Teeth pieces from your white fleece using the template. With right sides together, machine sew them along the lines marked on your pattern. Turn the right sides out and sew them again along the lines marked on the pattern to create detail. Depending on how much of the teeth you would like showing, pin them in place and hand sew them to the inside brim.

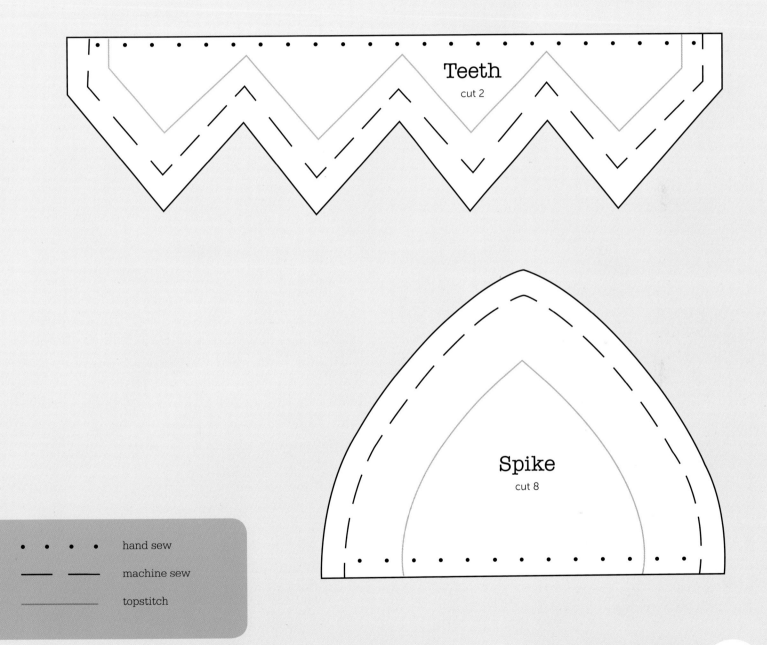

Teeth
cut 2

Spike
cut 8

· · · · · hand sew

— — — machine sew

——— topstitch

Dinosaur Bag

This bag is so cute, it's great to have around with or without the matching hat!

Tools and Materials

- Basic Sewing Tool Kit (page 9)
- ½ yard (45.7 cm) of green fleece (solid or tie-dyed)
- ⅛ yard (11.4 cm) of brown fleece
- 9 feet (2.7 m) of polyester cording
- Polyester fiberfill

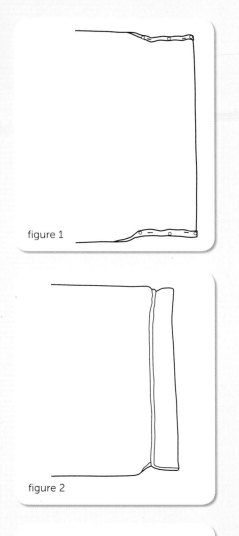

figure 1

figure 2

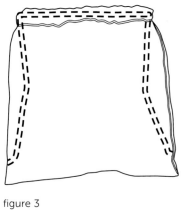

figure 3

Instructions

1 Cut your green fleece into a 15 x 34-inch (38.1 x 86.4 cm) rectangle using your rotary cutter, grid, and mat. Be careful as you cut to make sure the piece has a 90° angle.

2 To create a finished edge along the opening of the drawstring channels, fold the fabric over (wrong side to wrong side) on the long sides ¼ inch (6 mm) at each corner for 4 inches (10.2 cm). Pin and sew the folded edges in place **(figure 1)**.

3 Fold the short end over 2 inches (5.1 cm), wrong side to wrong side, and sew it to create a channel. Repeat this on the other short side of the fabric **(figure 2)**.

4 Cut the cording into two 53-inch (1.3 m) sections. To prevent your cording from fraying, carefully singe all ends with a flame to melt the fibers together.

5 Fold your fabric in half, with right sides facing, so the channels are together at the top. String the ends of one piece of cording through each channel and repeat this step for the other cording coming from the other direction. You should now be able to gather the top of the bag together.

6 Making sure the cording is not twisted, sandwich each end between the two fabric sections with ½ inch (1.3 cm) of the string sticking out of the side 1 inch (2.5 cm) up from the bottom corner of the bag. Pin the sides and cording in place and repeat these steps for the other side of the bag. Sew along the two edges from the bottom corners up to the channels **(figure 3)**. Do not sew over the channels; they need to stay open so the drawstring can move through them. Turn your bag right side out.

7 Cut eight Spike pieces out of brown fleece using the template. With right sides together, sew along the curves of the spike as marked on the template, leaving the straight edge unfinished. Turn the spike right side out and topstitch ⅝ inch (1.6 cm) from the outer edge following the markings on the pattern. Repeat the sewing instructions in this step to create three more spikes.

8 Fold your bag in half lengthwise to find the middle. Draw a line in chalk or mark it with pins so you can attach your spikes in a straight line. Stuff the inside of each spike with fiberfill and hand sew them on the bag, starting the first spike at the top of the bag and working down toward the bottom.

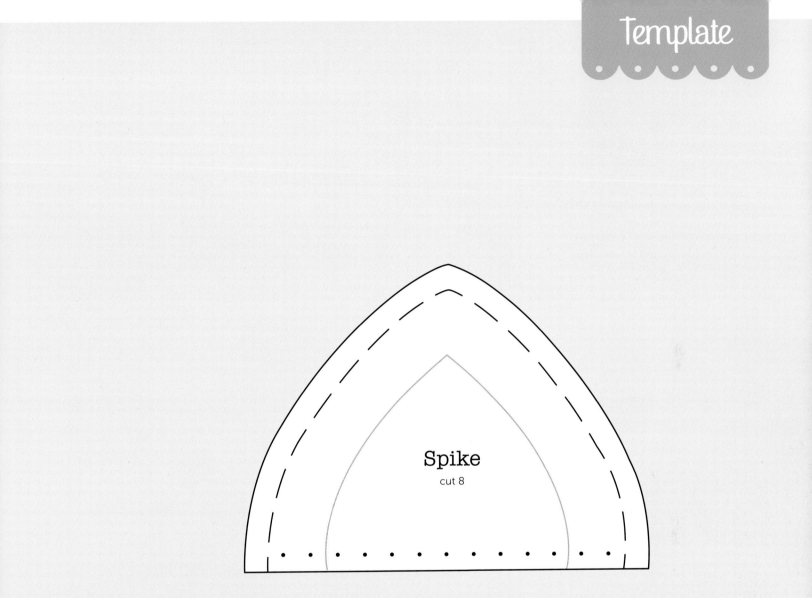

Spike

cut 8

· · · · ·   hand sew

— — —   machine sew

————   topstitch

Tall Giraffe

Your kids will seem to grow as soon as they put on this hat!

Tools and Materials

- Basic Sewing Tool Kit (page 9)
- ¼ yard (22.9 cm) of gold fleece
- ¼ yard (22.9 cm) of brown fleece
- Polyester fiberfill
- Black beads, fleece, polyester fiberfill for eyes

{ If you're using 9 x 12-inch (22.9 x 30.5 cm) sheets of fleece, you will need 3 sheets of gold fleece and 4 sheets of brown fleece. }

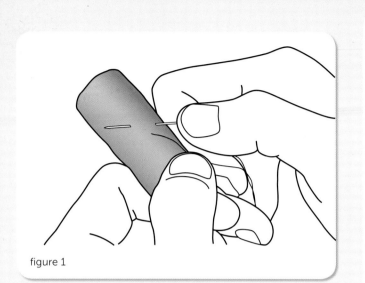

figure 1

Instructions

1 Using the instructions and templates for the Basic Hat (page 10), create your hat using gold fleece for the top of the hat and brown for the brim.

2 Topstitch ¼ inch (6 mm) down from the top edge of the brim to secure it in place.

3 Cut two Ossicone Base pieces from your gold fleece using the template. (I thought I would use the correct terminology instead of calling them giraffe "horns.") Roll this base piece like you are rolling up a sleeping bag, then sew along the straight edge to keep the roll from unfolding, as shown in **figure 1**. Roll and sew the second piece to create the second Ossicone Base.

4 Cut two Ossicone Top pieces from brown fleece using the template. Baste stitch around the outer edge of one circle and pull the thread to create a pouch. Stuff a small amount of fiberfill in this pouch, cinch the pouch shut, and sew the opening closed. Repeat this step to make the second Ossicone Top. Hand stitch the tops to the bases.

5 Cut two Ear pieces out of gold fleece and two Ear pieces out of brown fleece. Place one gold piece and one brown piece with right sides together, and sew around the two curved edges of the ear, leaving the straight section open as marked on the pattern. Turn the ear right side out and topstitch along the two curved edges ⅝ inch (1.6 cm) from the edge. Repeat these sewing instructions for the second ear.

6 Attach the ossicones on either side of the hat about 1 inch (2.5 cm) from the center seam. Attach the ears on either side of the hat below the ossicones.

7 Select the type of eyes you would like from the Basics section (page 14). Attach the eyes just above the brim on the front of the hat.

8 Cut one Spot of each size from brown fleece using the templates and attach them using a ladder stitch where desired.

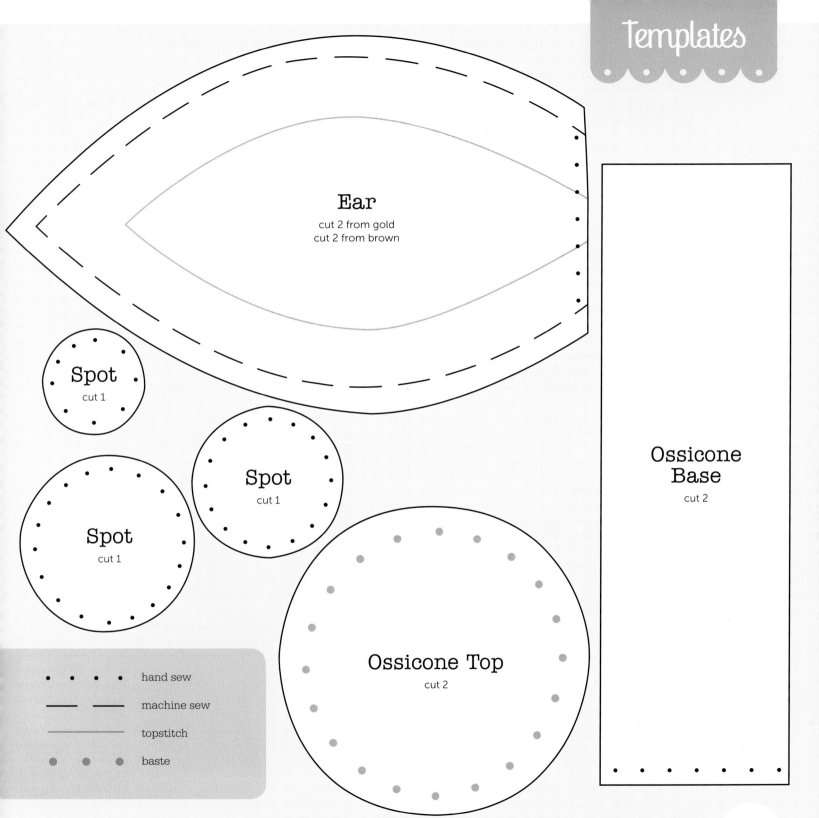

Ear

cut 2 from gold
cut 2 from brown

Spot

cut 1

Spot

cut 1

Spot

cut 1

Ossicone Top

cut 2

Ossicone Base

cut 2

• • • • hand sew

— – — machine sew

——— topstitch

● ● ● baste

Giraffe Scarf

What do giraffes use to keep their necks warm? Probably a scarf like this one!

Tools and Materials

- Basic Sewing Tool Kit (page 9)
- ½ yard (45.7 cm) of gold fleece
- ¼ yard (22.9 cm) of dark brown fleece

Sizes of Cut Fleece

XS/S:

- Two 7 x 42-inch (17.8 x 106.7 cm) pieces of gold fleece
- Four 4 x 5½-inch (10.2 x 14 cm) pieces of dark brown fleece

M/L:

- Two 8 x 54-inch (20.3 x 137.2 cm) pieces of gold fleece
- Four 5 x 6½-inch (12.7 x 16.5 cm) pieces of dark brown fleece

Instructions

1 Using your rotary cutter, grid, and mat, cut the gold fleece into two rectangles with the appropriate dimensions listed on page 52. Be careful to make the corner angles square as you cut.

2 With right sides facing, pin the two pieces together and sew a ¼-inch (6 mm) seam down the long edges of each side. Turn the project right side out and topstitch ¼ inch (6 mm) from the edges on the long sides for a finished edge.

3 Using your rotary cutter, grid, and mat, cut the dark brown fleece into four rectangles with the appropriate dimensions listed. Leaving ½ inch (1.3 cm) uncut on the long edge of each dark brown rectangle, cut ½-inch (1.3 cm) fringes down the length of the pieces. With wrong sides facing each other, sew two rectangles together ¼ inch (6 mm) from the uncut long edge and repeat this step for the second set. Tuck ½ inch (1.3 cm) of the uncut dark brown fleece into the openings at the ends of the scarf and pin them in place. Machine sew along the short edges of the scarf to secure the fringe in place.

4 Cut two circles of each size from your dark brown fleece using the Spot templates. Using one spot of each size, sew them to each end of the scarf using a ladder stitch. Catch the top layer only; be sure to not let your stitching go through to the other side of the scarf.

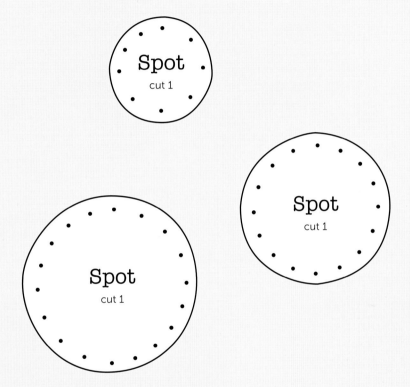

Spot
cut 1

Spot
cut 1

Spot
cut 1

• • • • • hand sew

Gone Fishing

This is one fish that feels just fine out of the pond.

Tools and Materials

- Basic Sewing Tool Kit (page 9)
- ½ yard (45.7 cm) of orange fleece
- Polyester fiberfill
- Black beads, fleece, polyester fiberfill for eyes

{ If you're using 9 x 12-inch (22.9 x 30.5 cm) sheets of fleece, you will need 8 sheets of orange fleece. }

Instructions

1 Using the instructions and templates for the Basic Hat (page 10), create your hat using orange fleece. (As with any pattern in this book, feel free to take liberties with colors.)

2 Cut two Top Fin, two Tail, and four Side Fin pieces using the templates. For each pair, be sure to cut one piece with the pattern facing up and one piece with the pattern facing down. Place each pair together with the right sides facing; sew along the curved edges as marked on the pattern, leaving the bottom edges open. Turn each of them right side out and sew along the detail lines marked on the pattern to create grooves in the fins and tail. In between each of these seams, stuff fiberfill so the fins have structure.

3 On the sides of your hat, tuck the bottom ½ inch (1.3 cm) of your side fins under the brim. Pin them in place and topstitch ¼ inch (6 mm) down from the top edge of the brim to secure the fins and the brim in place. Your machine will be going through many layers of fleece and some fiberfill when going over the fins, so guide the hat through carefully.

4 At the top of your hat, you will see an X formed by the seams. Place the front edge of your tail on this X and let the rest follow along the seam that runs to the back of the hat. Sew one side of the tail to the hat, following the contours where the tail swells from fiberfill, and continue to do the same on the other side. Make sure to stitch tightly so the stitches sink into the fleece; this will also keep the tail upright. You have stitched it correctly if the tail sticks up when someone is wearing the hat.

5 Place the back of the top fin so it touches the front of the tail, and follow the seam running to the front of the hat. Just as you did with the tail, sew one side of the fin in place following its contours and continue around to the other side, pulling the stitches tight. To further stabilize the top fin, sew the top fin and tail together right at the point where they touch.

6 Select the type of eyes you would like from the Basics section (page 14). Attach the eyes just above the brim on the front of the hat.

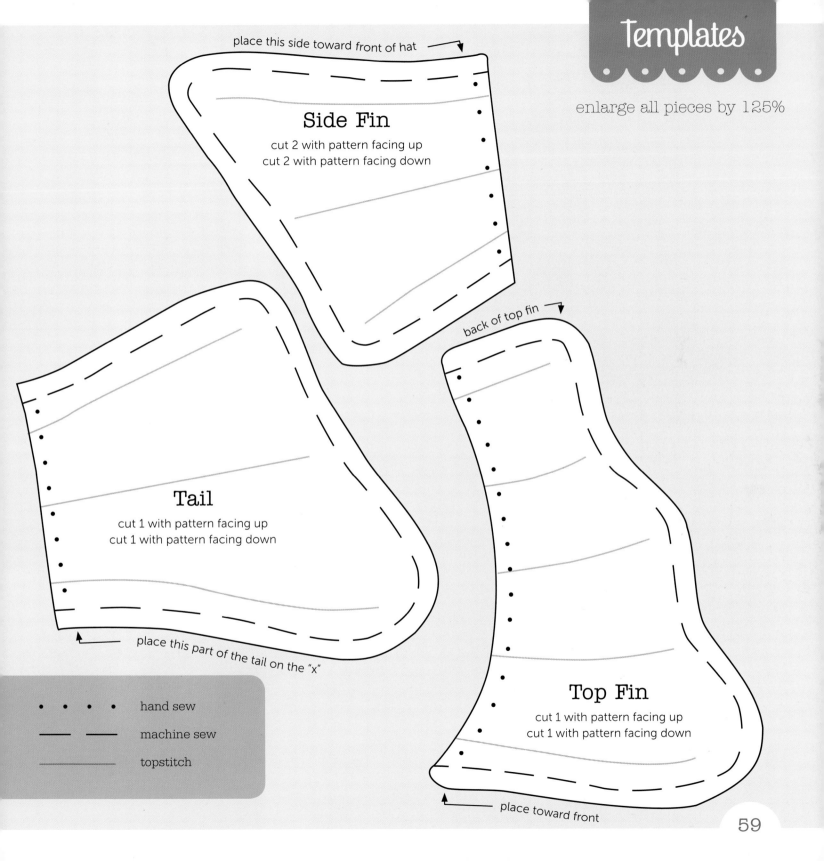

place this side toward front of hat

Side Fin
cut 2 with pattern facing up
cut 2 with pattern facing down

back of top fin

Tail
cut 1 with pattern facing up
cut 1 with pattern facing down

place this part of the tail on the "x"

Top Fin
cut 1 with pattern facing up
cut 1 with pattern facing down

place toward front

· · · · ·   hand sew

— — —   machine sew

————   topstitch

59

Happy as a Hippo

The flared nostrils make this hat the silliest on the savanna.

Tools and Materials

- Basic Sewing Tool Kit (page 9)
- ¼ yard (22.9 cm) of violet fleece
- Scrap of white fleece
- Black beads, fleece, polyester fiberfill for eyes

{ If you're using 9 x 12-inch (22.9 x 30.5 cm) sheets of fleece you will need 6 sheets of violet fleece and 1 sheet or scrap of white fleece }

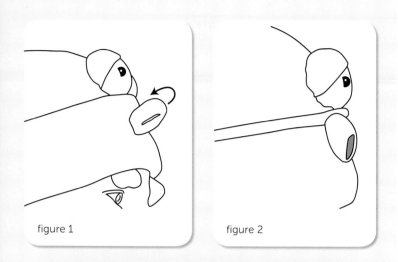

figure 1   figure 2

Instructions

1 Using the instructions and templates for the Basic Hat (page 10), create your hat using violet fleece.

2 Topstitch ¼ inch (6 mm) down from the top edge of the brim to secure it in place.

3 Cut four Nostril pieces from violet fleece using the template. Place two pieces with right sides together and sew along the curved edge marked on the pattern, leaving the straight edge open. Turn the piece so the right sides are facing out. Fold the unfinished straight edge of the nose in half. Hand sew the unfinished edge together. Repeat these sewing instructions to create a second nostril. Attach the flat part of the nostrils onto the brim so the pieces are sticking straight out **(figure 1)**. Next, fold back the tips of the nostrils and hand sew their edges to the hat **(figure 2)**.

4 Select the type of eyes you would like from the Basics section (page 14). Attach the eyes above the brim on the front of the hat.

5 Cut four Ear pieces from violet fleece using the template. Place two pieces with right sides together and sew along the curved edge as marked on the pattern, leaving the straight edge open. Turn the piece so the right sides are facing out. Fold the unfinished straight edge of the ear in half. Hand sew the unfinished edge together. Repeat these sewing instructions to create the second ear. Pin the ears on each side of the hat, with the folds facing forward, and sew them in place.

6 Cut four Tooth pieces from white fleece using the template. Place two pieces with right sides together and sew along the three edges marked on the pattern, leaving the top edge open. When finished, turn the right sides out. Repeat the sewing instructions to create a second tooth. Depending on how much of the teeth you would like showing, pin them on the inside of the brim and hand sew them in place.

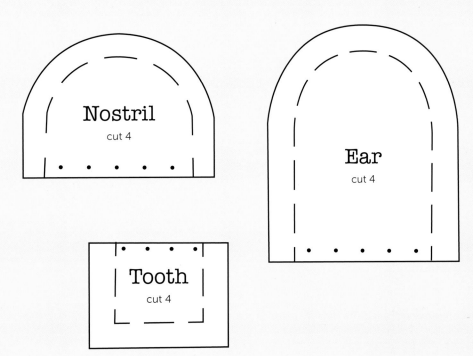

Nostril
cut 4

Ear
cut 4

Tooth
cut 4

• • • •   hand sew

———   machine sew

Little Ladybug

Make this hat for the lucky lady in your life.

Tools and Materials

- Basic Sewing Tool Kit (page 9)
- ¼ yard (22.9 cm) of red fleece
- ¼ yard (22.9 cm) of black fleece
- 1 pipe cleaner
- Two ½ inch (1.3 cm) black pom-poms
- Black beads, fleece, polyester fiberfill for eyes

{ If you're using 9 x 12-inch (22.9 x 30.5 cm) sheets of fleece, you will need 2 sheets of red fleece and 4 sheets of black fleece. }

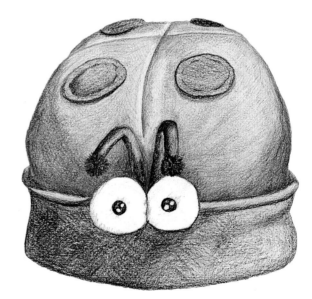

Instructions

1 Using the instructions and templates for the Basic Hat (page 10), create your hat using red fleece for the top and black fleece for the brim.

2 Create the antennas by cutting the pipe cleaner to 8 inches (20.3 cm) in length. Cut one Antenna piece out of black fleece using the template. Wrap the fleece around your pipe cleaner and ladder stitch along all the edges. Hand sew a pom-pom on each end of the antenna. Form the antenna into a V shape and bend the ends forward slightly.

3 Tuck the bottom ½ inch (1.3 cm) of the point on the V under the brim. Pin it in place and topstitch a seam ¼ inch (6 mm) down from the top edge of the brim to secure the brim and the antenna in place.

4 Select the type of eyes you would like from the Basics section (page 14). Attach the eyes overlapping the brim on the front of the hat.

Note: Play around with the placement of the eyes and antennas before attaching them so you do not end up with an angry-looking ladybug!

5 Cut four Spot pieces from your black fleece using the template. Pin all four spots where desired and hand stitch them in place using a ladder stitch.

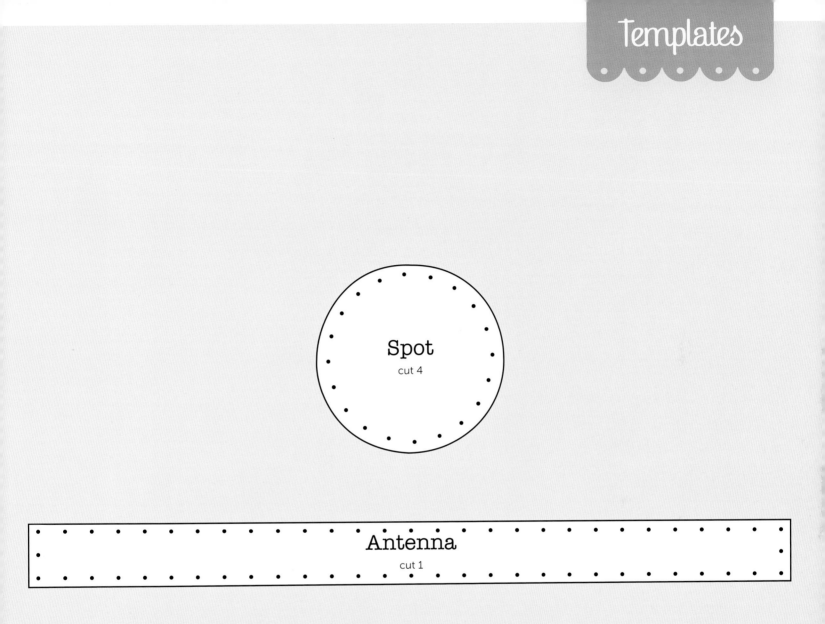

Spot
cut 4

Antenna
cut 1

• • • • • hand sew

Lion Around

With such a regal mane, anyone who wears this hat has plenty of pride.

Tools and Materials

- Basic Sewing Tool Kit (page 9)
- ¼ yard (22.9 cm) of tan fleece
- ¼ yard (22.9 cm) of off-white fleece
- Scrap of pale yellow fleece
- Scrap of black fleece
- ⅓ yard (22.9 cm) of dark brown fleece
- Black beads for eyes

{ If using 9 x 12-inch (22.9 x 30.5 cm) sheets of fleece, you will need 3 sheets of tan fleece, 4 sheets of off-white fleece, 1 sheet or scrap of pale yellow fleece, 1 sheet or scrap of black fleece, and 7 sheets of dark brown fleece. }

Instructions

1 Using the instructions and templates for the Basic Hat (page 10), create your hat using tan fleece for the top of the hat and off-white for the brim.

2 Topstitch ¼ inch (6 mm) down from the top edge of the brim to secure it in place.

3 Cut one Top of Nose piece from pale yellow fleece and one Bottom of Nose piece from black fleece using the templates. Place the Top of Nose piece just above the brim, centered along the vertical seam, and hand sew it in place. Line up the black Bottom of Nose piece so the top two corners of this piece match up with the bottom corners on the Top of Nose triangle. Hand sew the Bottom of Nose on the brim in this spot.

4 Cut two Ear pieces from off-white fleece and two from tan fleece using the template. Place one tan piece and one off-white piece with right sides together and sew around the curved edge as marked on the pattern, leaving the straight section open. Repeat this step for the second ear. Flip the ears right side out and fold the unfinished edge of the ear in half. Hand sew the unfinished edge together and attach them on each side of the hat, with the off-white sides facing forward.

5 Select the type of eyes you would like from the Basics section (page 14). Attach the eyes up from the brim on the front of the hat.

6 Cut 4½-inch-wide (11.4 cm) strips as long as possible from dark brown fleece and fold the wrong sides together. Baste stitch the edges together. Lay your pieces flat on your mat and cut from the folded edge toward the seam every inch (2.5 cm) using your grid and rotary cutter. Leave about ¼ inch (6 mm) at the seam edge to keep the pieces together. Prepare 3⅓ to 4 yards (3 to 3.7 m) of mane strips to start (note that this is not a continuous piece). The actual length you need depends on how close you sew your strips onto the hat.

7 Attach the strips starting on one side of the face at the bottom of the brim, going up the seam on the side of the hat, around the back of the ears, and back down the other side. Begin stitching each strip in place, filling the rest of the space by using whatever pattern you prefer.

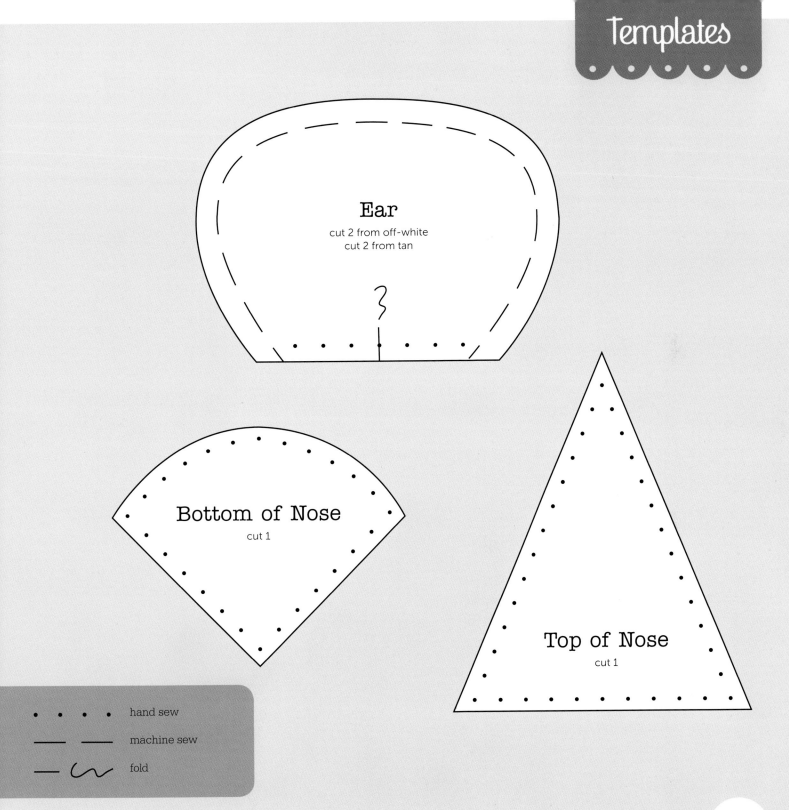

Ear

cut 2 from off-white
cut 2 from tan

Bottom of Nose

cut 1

Top of Nose

cut 1

• • • • • hand sew

—— —— machine sew

— ∿ fold

Tails

You can easily change this basic tail's length or color to match your favorite hat!

Tools and Materials

- Basic Sewing Tool Kit (page 9)
- Giraffe Tail: ⅛ yard (11.4 cm) of gold fleece and ⅛ yard (11.4 cm) of brown fleece
- Lion Tail: ⅛ yard (11.4 cm) of tan fleece and ¼ yard (22.9 cm) of dark brown fleece
- Polyester fiberfill
- 1 alligator clip per tail

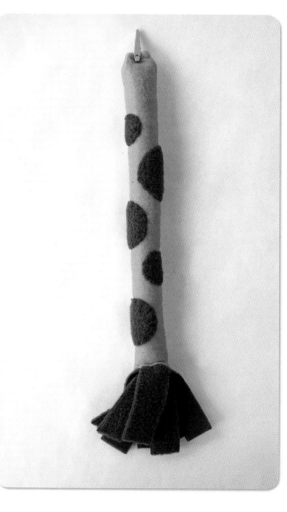

Instructions

1 Using the template, cut one Tail piece out of the first color listed for your desired animal tail. Fold it in half the long way with right sides together and sew along the marked edge. Turn this piece so the right side is facing out.

2 For the giraffe, use the template to cut one Fringe piece out of the second color listed for your desired animal tail. Cut along the marked lines on the pattern to create fringe, leaving ½ inch (1.3 cm) uncut at the top of each block.

For the lion, refer to step 6 of the Lion Around hat pattern on page 70 to make 8 inches (20.3 cm) of lion mane for the fringe.

3 Roll the fringe piece like a sleeping bag with the right sides facing out. Sew a few stitches along the uncut end of the roll to keep the layers from slipping. Stuff the roll into one end of the tube and hand sew it in place.

4 Stuff fiberfill in the tube leaving the top ½ inch (1.3 cm) unstuffed. Gather the end of the tube slightly until it is closed.

5 The giraffe has prints on its tail. To create the print pattern, cut five Spots of various sizes using the templates that accompany the Tall Giraffe hat pattern on page 51 and sew them onto the tail using a ladder stitch.

6 Sew one alligator clip at the top of the tail, making sure it is secure.

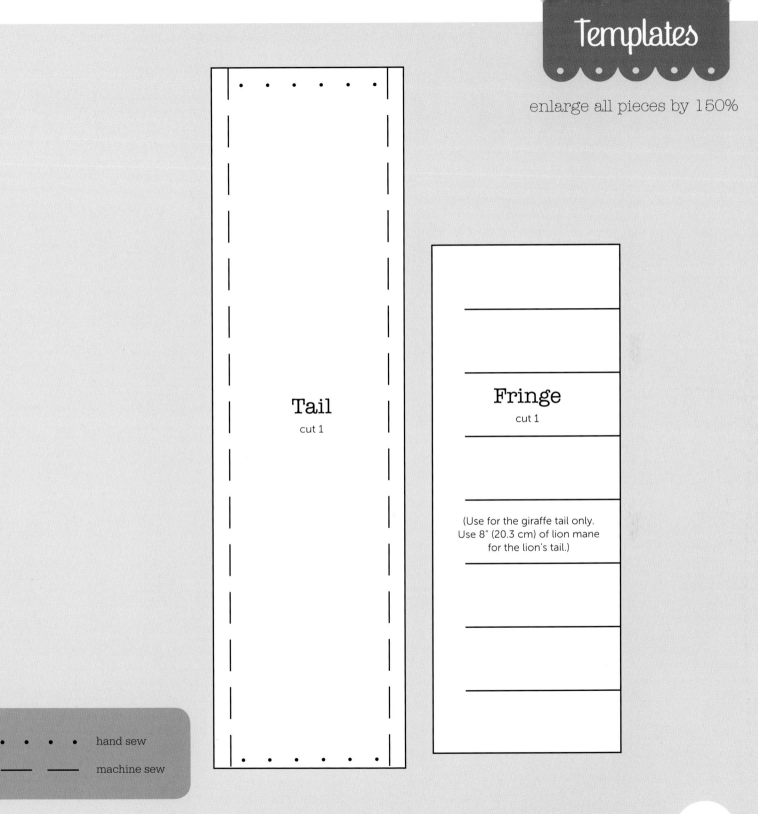

Tail

cut 1

Fringe

cut 1

(Use for the giraffe tail only.
Use 8" (20.3 cm) of lion mane
for the lion's tail.)

• • • • • •   hand sew

— — — — —   machine sew

Under the Sea

A fine hat for a seaside vacation—dreaming of summer trips to the beach.

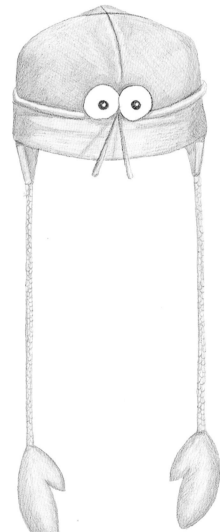

Tools and Materials

- Basic Sewing Tool Kit (page 9)
- ½ yard (45.7 cm) of red fleece
- 1 pipe cleaner
- Black beads, fleece, polyester fiberfill for eyes
- Polyester fiberfill

If you're using 9 x 12-inch (22.9 x 30.5 cm) sheets of fleece you will need 9 sheets of red fleece.

Instructions

1 Using the instructions and templates for the Basic Hat (page 10), create your hat using red fleece.

2 Topstitch ¼ inch (6 mm) down from the top edge of the brim to secure it in place.

3 Cut a ⅝-inch-wide (1.6 cm) piece of red fleece the length of your pipe cleaner. Wrap it around the pipe cleaner and ladder stitch along all the edges. Form the antenna into a large V shape. Center and sew the point of the antenna V on the front of the hat just above the brim. (Although we often think that antennas belong above the eyes, such as they are with bees and ladybugs, lobster antennas are actually below their eyes at the most-forward spot on their face.)

4 Select the type of eyes you would like from Basics section (page 14). Hand sew the eyes on directly above the antennas.

5 Refer to the Earflaps, Braids, and Tassels instructions in the Basics section (page 12) to make these features, which are the "arms" of your lobster.

6 Cut four Claw pieces from the template, making sure to cut two with the pattern facing up and two with the pattern facing down. Place two together with right sides facing and sew around the edges leaving a 1-inch (2.5 cm) opening at the wrist of the lobster as marked on the pattern. Repeat this step for the second claw.

7 Turn both claws right side out. Loosely stuff fiberfill in the claws, which on the American lobster are called chelipeds. (Thank goodness you made this project—you are now so much more knowledgeable!)

8 Place the end of your tassel braid into the opening of the cheliped and machine sew across the openings. Repeat this step for the other side.

Note: Make sure both claw "thumbs" are facing forward.

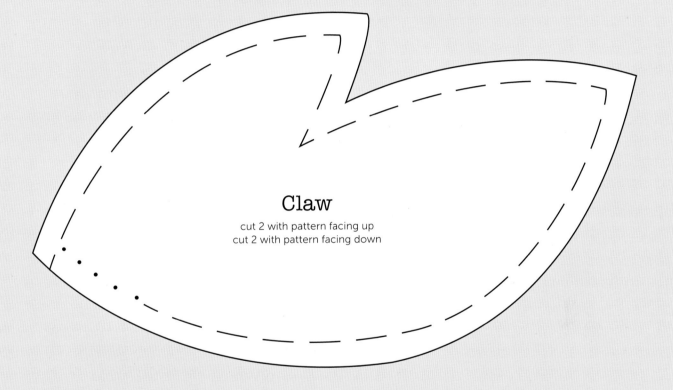

Claw

cut 2 with pattern facing up
cut 2 with pattern facing down

. . . . . hand sew

——— ——— machine sew

Monkeying Around

Does your little one get into monkey business? I have just the hat...

Tools and Materials

- Basic Sewing Tool Kit (page 9)
- ¼ yard (22.9 cm) of dark brown fleece
- ¼ yard (22.9 cm) of off-white fleece
- Scrap of medium brown fleece
- Polyester fiberfill
- Black beads for eyes
- Black embroidery floss

{ If you're using 9 x 12-inch (22.9 x 30.5 cm) sheets of fleece you will need 3 sheets of dark brown fleece, 4 sheets of off-white fleece, and 1 sheet or scrap of medium brown fleece. }

Instructions

1 Using the instructions and templates for the Basic Hat (page 10), create your hat using dark brown fleece for the top and off-white fleece for the brim.

2 Cut two Face pieces from off-white fleece using the template. With right sides together, sew along the edges as marked on the pattern, leaving the straight edge open. Turn your piece so the right sides are facing out and sew around the curved edge once again, only this time topstitching ⅝ inch (1.6 cm) from the outer edge. Center the Face piece on the front of the hat and tuck ½ inch (1.3 cm) of the unfinished edge under the hat's front brim and pin it in place. Attach the top edge of this piece to the dark brown fleece by following the topstitching again with your machine (also called stitching in the ditch).

3 Topstitch ¼ inch (6 mm) down from the top edge of the brim to secure it in place.

4. Cut one Top of Mouth piece and one Bottom of Mouth piece from off-white fleece using the templates. With right sides together, sew the bottom curve of the Top of Mouth piece to the top curve of the Bottom of Mouth piece. Turn this right side out and center it below the monkey Face piece under the seam on the brim. Hand sew it in place; add a fair amount of fiberfill as you near the end of your stitching.

5 Cut one Nose piece from a scrap of medium brown fleece. Fold it in half lengthwise to create a small tube and then sew it on the seam on the brim, centered on the face.

6 Select the type of eyes you would like from the Basics section (page 14). Attach the eyes just above the brim on the front of the hat.

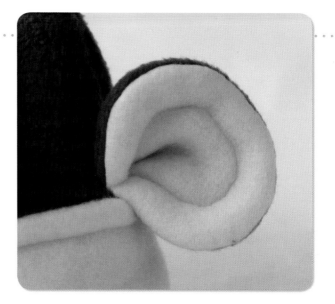

7 Using black embroidery floss, hand stitch along the "smiling" mouth seam and stitch eyebrows above the eyes if desired.

8 Cut two Ear pieces out of dark brown fleece and two Ear pieces out of off-white fleece using the template. Place one of each color with right sides together and sew along the curved edge of the ear as marked on your pattern, leaving the straight section open. Turn your ear right side out and sew along the curved edge of the ear, topstitching ½ inch (1.3 cm) from the edge. Repeat these sewing instructions for the second ear.

9 Take the unfinished edge of the ear and fold it in half so the off-white side is on the inside of the fold. Hand sew the unfinished edge together. Repeat this step for the other ear. Pin the ears on each side of the hat, above the brim, with the off-white sides facing forward. Sew them in place.

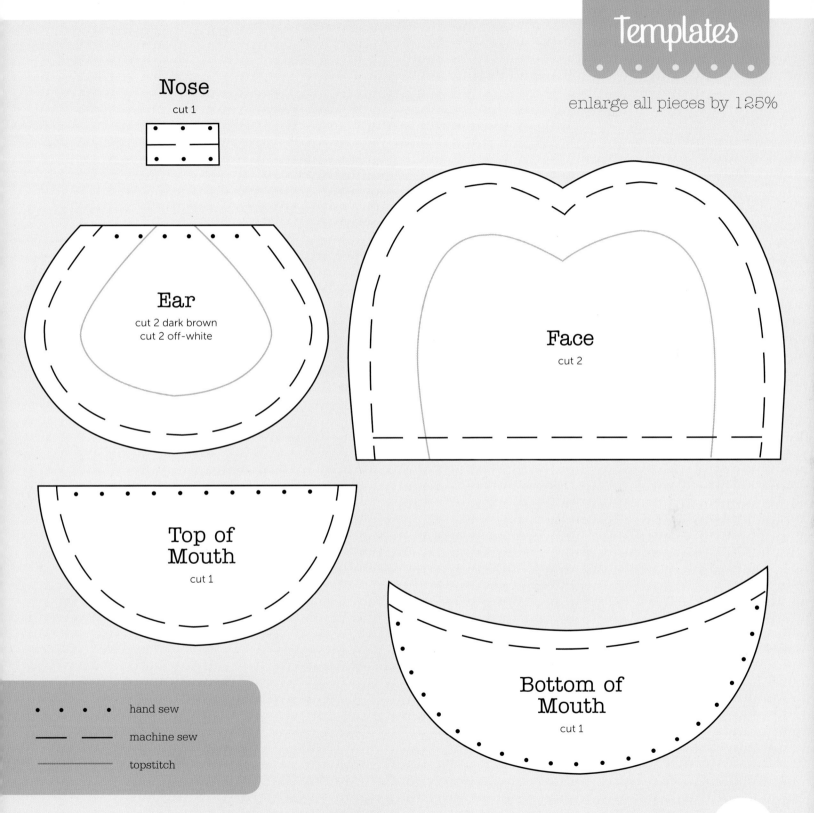

enlarge all pieces by 125%

Nose

cut 1

Ear

cut 2 dark brown
cut 2 off-white

Face

cut 2

Top of
Mouth

cut 1

Bottom of
Mouth

cut 1

• • • • •   hand sew

— — — —   machine sew

————————   topstitch

Monkey Sweatshirt

Grab the boring hoodie hanging in the closet and go a little wild with it!

Tools and Materials

- Basic Sewing Tool Kit (page 9)
- Solid-color hooded sweatshirt (hoodie)
- ¼ yard (22.9 cm) of brown fleece

Instructions

1 Spread out the sweatshirt on a table or flat surface and measure across the back from one side to the other. Determine where the middle is and mark it with chalk or pins. This will help when centering the tail.

2 Cut out the Tail piece from brown fleece using the template. Pin it to the back of your sweatshirt, starting the bottom of the tail at the bottom edge of the ribbing.

Note: The pattern in the book is for an Extra-Small or Small sweatshirt. If you are sewing this tail on a Medium or Large sweatshirt, you will need to extend the bottom of the tail. To do so, have someone try on the sweatshirt to determine how far down the hood falls. Mark this point with a safety pin and place another pin 2 inches (5.1 cm) below it. Measure from the lowest safety pin to the bottom edge of the ribbing. Subtract 10¼ inches (26 cm) from your measurement. The difference is how much longer you need the tail to be.

3 Lay the sweatshirt flat on a table and hand sew around the whole tail using a ladder stitch. Remember to remove all the pins before letting anyone monkey around in their new garb!

A wildly wonderful tip: When sewing the tail on the sweatshirt, place a flexible cutting board inside the sweatshirt to avoid sewing through to the front of the sweatshirt.

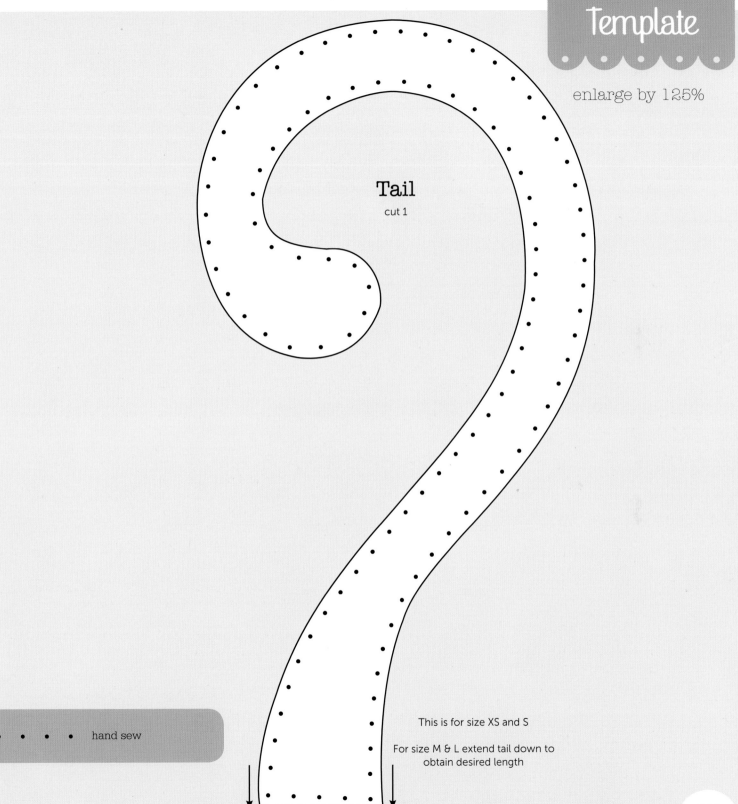

enlarge by 125%

Tail
cut 1

This is for size XS and S

For size M & L extend tail down to
obtain desired length

• • • • • hand sew

Monster Mash

This monster is ready for a Halloween party!

Tools and Materials

- Basic Sewing Tool Kit (page 9)
- ½ yard (45.7 cm) of green fleece
- Scrap of white fleece
- ⅛ yard (11.4 cm) of blue fleece
- Polyester fiberfill
- Black beads, fleece, polyester fiberfill for eye

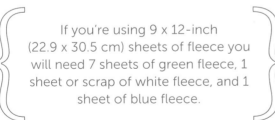

If you're using 9 x 12-inch (22.9 x 30.5 cm) sheets of fleece you will need 7 sheets of green fleece, 1 sheet or scrap of white fleece, and 1 sheet of blue fleece.

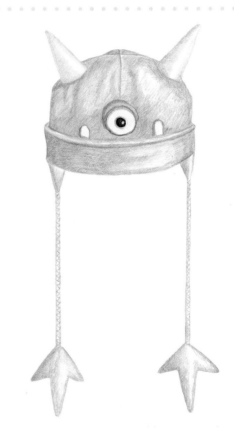

Instructions

1 Using the instructions and templates for the Basic Hat (page 10), create your hat using green fleece.

2 Cut two Tooth pieces out of white fleece using the template. Roll one piece and sew the loose edge in place. Choose one end to be the top. To make this end look like a rounded tooth, pull the top front layer over the spiral and sew it in place. Repeat these sewing instructions for the next tooth. Tuck ½ inch (1.3 cm) of each tooth under the brim of the hat (making sure each is about 2 inches (5.1 cm) off the center front of the hat) and pin in place.

3 Topstitch ¼ inch (6 mm) down from the top edge of the brim to secure the brim and teeth.

4 Go to the Earflaps, Braids, and Tassels instructions in the Basics section (page 12) to make these features, which will be the "arms" of your monster.

5 Cut four Hand pieces from your green fleece using the template. Place two pieces with right sides together, and sew along the lines marked on the pattern, leaving the straight edge open. Repeat this step for the second hand. Flip the hands right side out and loosely stuff them with fiberfill.

6 Place the end of one tassel braid into the opening of one hand and machine sew across it to secure. Repeat this step for the other hand.

7 Select the type of eye you would like from the Basics section (page 14). Sew the eye in place on the front of the hat, leaving some space between the eye and the brim.

8 Cut two Horn pieces from blue fleece using the template. Fold one piece as marked on the pattern so the right sides are together. Sew along the straight edge, leaving the rounded part of the cone open. Turn the horn right side out and loosely stuff it with fiberfill. Repeat this step to create the second horn. Hand sew the horns on either side of the hat. Be sure the horn seams are facing the back of the hat.

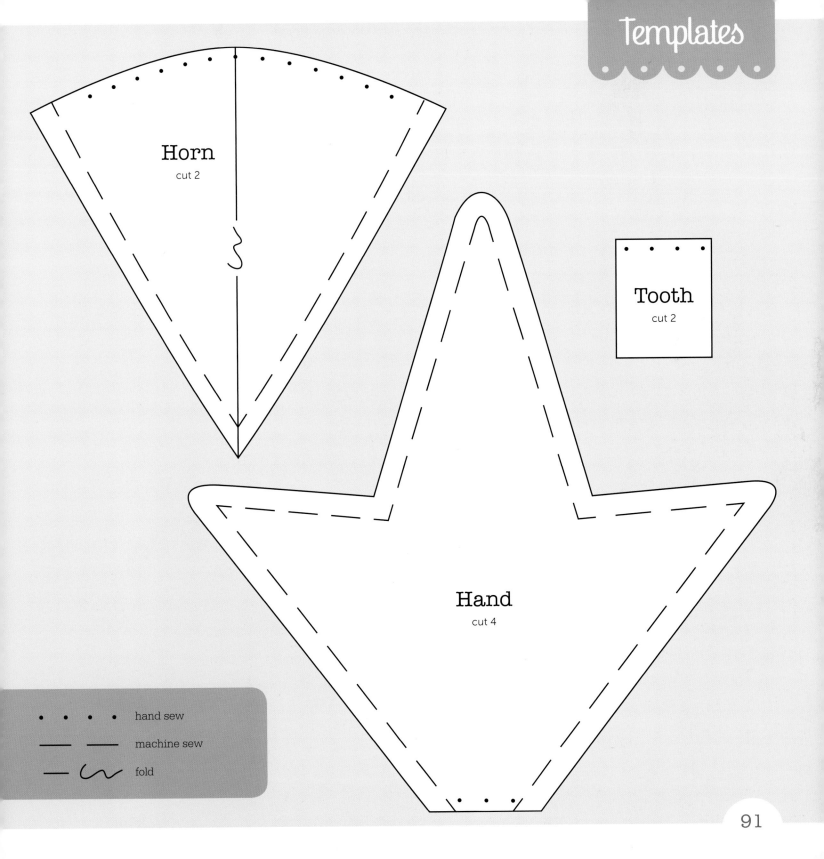

Horn
cut 2

Tooth
cut 2

Hand
cut 4

- • • • • hand sew
- ——— machine sew
- —⌇ fold

Mouse in the House

This one is always on the hunt for cheese.

Tools and Materials

- Basic Sewing Tool Kit (page 9)
- ¼ yard (22.9 cm) of dark blue fleece (solid or tie-dyed)
- ⅛ yard (11.4 cm) of gray fleece
- Polyester fiberfill
- Black beads for eyes and nose
- Black fishing line

{ If you're using 9 x 12-inch (22.9 x 30.5 cm) sheets of fleece, you will need 6 sheets of dark blue fleece (solid or tie-dyed) and 2 sheets of gray fleece. }

Instructions

1 Using the instructions and templates for the Basic Hat (page 10), create your hat using tie-dyed or solid blue fleece.

2 Topstitch ¼ inch (6 mm) down from the top edge of the brim to secure it in place.

3 Cut two Body pieces and one Bottom piece out of gray fleece using the template. Place the two Body pieces with right sides together and machine sew along the curved edge, leaving the straight edge open. With right sides together, line up the Bottom piece to the Body piece. Sew along the markings on the pattern, leaving an opening at the back end of the mouse. Turn right side out and fill the body with fiberfill until it is firm. Hand stitch this opening shut.

4 Cut four Ear pieces out of gray fleece, two with the template facing up and two with the template facing down. Match two pieces, place the right sides together, and sew along the curved edge of the ear as marked on the pattern, leaving the straight edge open. Turn the ear so the right sides are now facing out and sew around the curved edge once again, topstitching ¼ inch (6 mm) from the edge. Repeat this step for the second ear. Hand sew both ears onto the mouse body one-third of the way back from point of the nose.

5 Select the type of eyes you would like from the Basics section (page 14). The one shown on page 93 has Beady Eyes. Sew the eyes on the face of the mouse and sew another black bead on the tip of the nose.

6 Cut one Tail piece out of gray fleece using the template. Fold the tail piece in half lengthwise as shown on the pattern and ladder stitch along the edges. Sew the tail on the back end of the mouse.

7 Cut two Front Paw pieces and two Back Paw pieces out of gray fleece using the template. Make sure to cut one of each pair with the pattern facing up and one of each pair with the pattern facing down. Hand sew them to your hat in any spot that you prefer to place the mouse. Stitch the body in place on the hat so the ends of the "arms" are covered by it.

8 Thread your needle with black fishing line and pull it through from one side of the nose and exit out the other side. Knot the fishing line on each side of the nose close to the fleece to keep the whiskers in place. Repeat this step two more times for three sets of two whiskers. Trim them to the desired length.

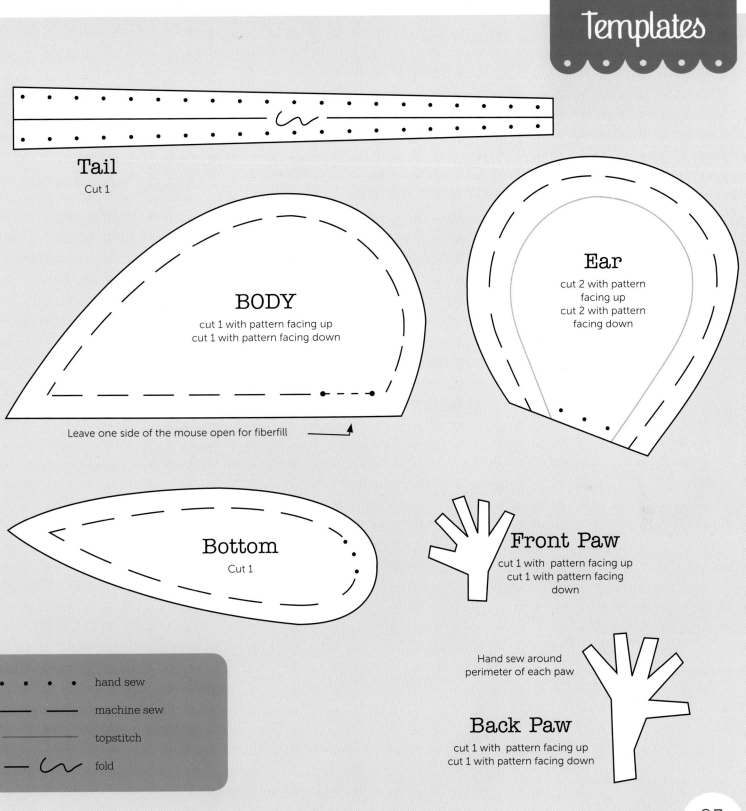

Tail

Cut 1

BODY

cut 1 with pattern facing up
cut 1 with pattern facing down

Leave one side of the mouse open for fiberfill

Ear

cut 2 with pattern
facing up
cut 2 with pattern
facing down

Bottom

Cut 1

Front Paw

cut 1 with pattern facing up
cut 1 with pattern facing
down

Hand sew around
perimeter of each paw

Back Paw

cut 1 with pattern facing up
cut 1 with pattern facing down

- • • • • hand sew
- ——— machine sew
- ——— topstitch
- — fold

A Real Hoot

Is there a night owl in your family?

Tools and Materials

- Basic Sewing Tool Kit (page 9)
- ¼ yard (22.9 cm) of aqua fleece
- ¼ yard (22.9 cm) of yellow fleece
- ⅛ yard (11.4 cm) of brown fleece
- Scrap of white fleece
- ⅛ yard (11.4 cm) of orange fleece
- Black beads and fleece for eyes

{ If you're using 9 x 12-inch (22.9 x 30.5 cm) sheets of fleece you will need 4 sheets of aqua fleece, 4 sheets of yellow fleece, 1 sheet of brown fleece, 1 sheet or scrap of white fleece, and 1 sheet of orange fleece. }

Instructions

1 Using the instructions and templates for the Basic Hat (page 10), create your hat using aqua fleece for the top of the hat and yellow fleece for the brim.

2 Topstitch ¼ inch (6 mm) down from the top edge of the brim to secure it in place.

3 Cut two Outer Eye pieces from brown fleece and two Inner Eye pieces from white fleece using the template. Center the two brown fleece pieces on the front of the hat, overlapping the brim, and hand sew them onto the hat using a ladder stitch. Center the white fleece circles on the brown fleece circles and hand sew them on, once again using a ladder stitch. The owl hat shown is made with beady eyes, but feel free to select another eye type from the Basics section (page 14); attach them in the middle of the white circles.

4 Cut one Nose from orange fleece using the template. Place the nose between the eyes, overlapping them, and sew it to the hat using a ladder stitch.

5 Cut four Ear pieces from aqua fleece using the template. Match two pieces with right sides together and machine sew along the outer edge of the ear as marked on your pattern, leaving the bottom of the triangle open. Turn the ear right side out. Repeat this step to create a second ear. Hand sew the ears on either side of the hat.

6 Cut two 1 x 5-inch (2.5 x 12.7 cm) strips from brown, yellow, and orange fleece. With one strip of each color, knot the group together in the middle and hand sew the tassel to the tip of the ear. Repeat these instructions for the second group of strips and the other ear.

7 Refer to the Earflaps, Braids, and Tassels instructions in the Basics section (page 12) to make these features using aqua fleece for the earflap and orange fleece for the braids and tassels.

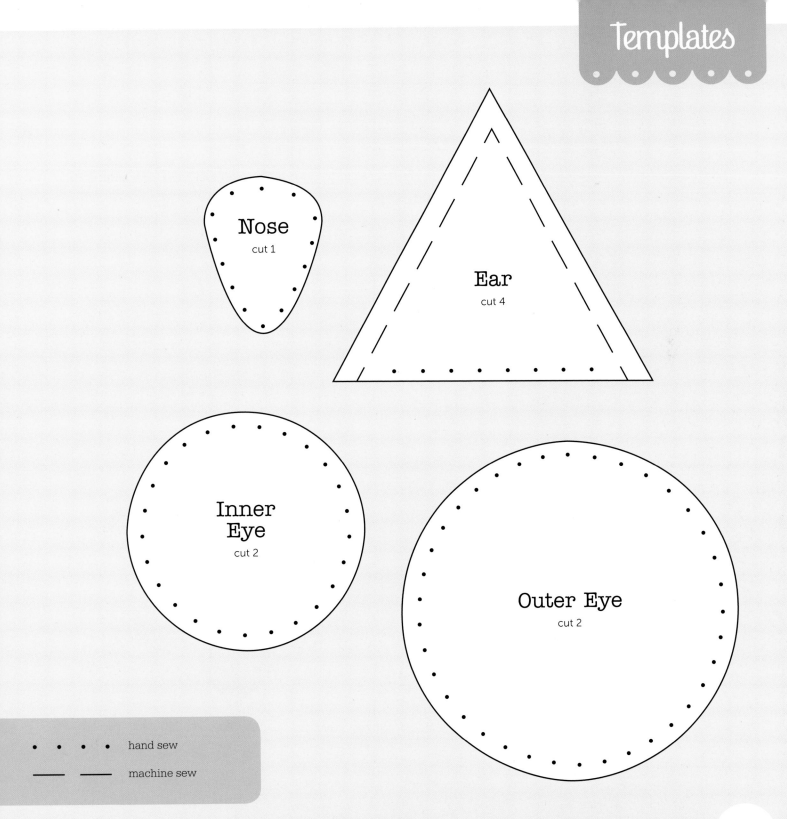

Nose
cut 1

Ear
cut 4

Inner Eye
cut 2

Outer Eye
cut 2

· · · · · hand sew

——— machine sew

Playful Panda

Forget bamboo—all this panda needs is you.

Tools and Materials

- Basic Sewing Tool Kit (page 9)
- ¼ yard (22.9 cm) of white fleece
- ⅛ yard (11.4 cm) of black fleece
- Black beads and fleece for eyes

{ If you're using 9 x 12-inch (22.9 x 30.5 cm) sheets of fleece, you will need 6 sheets of white fleece and 1 sheet of black fleece. }

Instructions

1 Using the instructions and templates for the Basic Hat (page 10), create your hat using white fleece.

2 Topstitch ¼ inch (6 mm) down from the top edge of the brim to secure it in place. To create the natural groove, or *philtrum*, that comes down from the panda's nose to its lips, use the vertical seam on the brim of your hat.

3 Cut four Ear pieces out of black fleece using the template, two with the pattern facing up and two with the pattern facing down. Match a pair with right sides together and sew along the curved edge, leaving the bottom edge open as marked on your pattern. Flip the ear right side out. Fold the ear in half along the line that is marked on the pattern and baste stitch along the straight edge to keep the ear fold in place. Repeat this step for the second ear and hand sew the ears on either side of the hat.

4 Cut one Nose piece out of black fleece using the template. Using a ladder stitch, sew it on the brim of your hat, centering it on the vertical seam and placing the top of the nose in line with the top edge of the brim.

5 Cut two Eye pieces out of black fleece using the template, one with the pattern facing up and one with the pattern facing down. Using a ladder stitch, hand sew each eye piece in place where desired. The example shown also has Beady Eyes from the Basics section (page 14). Attach the eyes on top of the eye pieces.

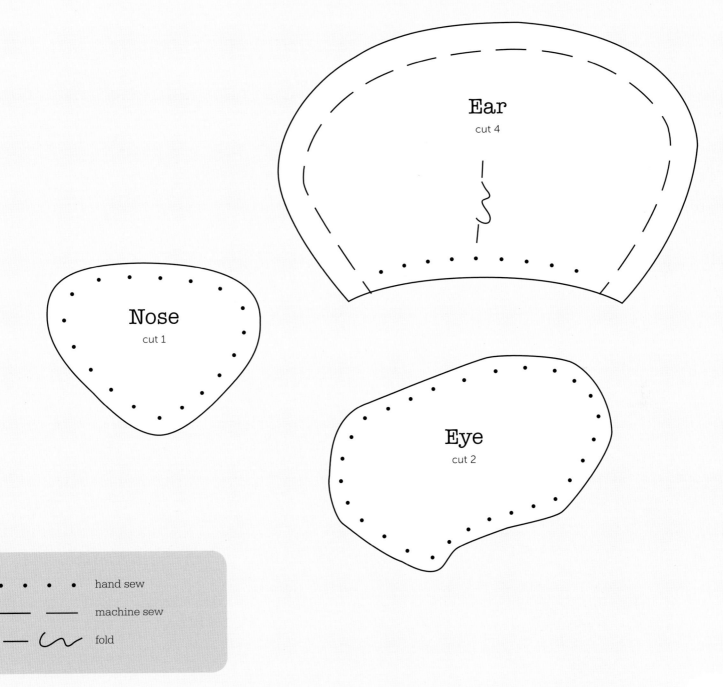

Ear
cut 4

Nose
cut 1

Eye
cut 2

• • • •   hand sew

———   machine sew

—ᘐᘕ—   fold

Waddling Penguin

A fine hat all winter long— no tuxedo required!

Tools and Materials

- Basic Sewing Tool Kit (page 9)
- ¼ yard (22.9 cm) of black fleece
- ¼ yard (22.9 cm) of white fleece
- ⅛ yard (11.4 cm) of yellow fleece
- Polyester fiberfill
- Black beads, fleece, polyester fiberfill for eyes

{ If you're using 9 x 12-inch (22.9 x 30.5 cm) sheets of fleece, you will need 5 sheets of black fleece, 6 sheets of white fleece, and 2 sheets of yellow fleece. }

Instructions

1 Using the instructions and templates for the Basic Hat (page 10), create your hat using black fleece for the top of your hat and white for the brim.

2 Cut two Face pieces from the white fleece using the template. With right sides together, sew from the bottom of the face piece up to the point on both outer edges. Refold the face piece with right sides together to create an arc. Make sure to pin the very top where the seams meet so they align perfectly, and sew along the arc. Turn the piece so the right sides are facing out. Lay it flat so the seams that go all the way to the bottom of the piece are on the sides and one of the short seams is directly in the middle. Now sew along the top curve of this piece ¼ inch (6 mm) from the outer edge.

3 Place the face piece on the hat so that it nests on the front, centering it between the side seams, and pin it in place. Stitch once again along the seam you just created on the face (also called stitching in the ditch), only this time securing it to the hat.

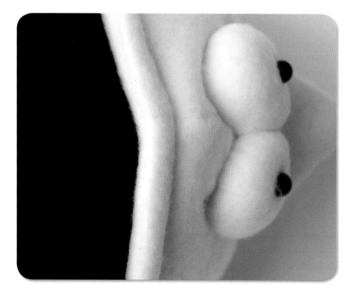

4 Flip the brim up over the white face piece, pin, and topstitch ¼ inch (6 mm) down from the top edge of the brim to secure it in place.

5 Cut two Beak pieces from yellow fleece using the template. With right sides together, sew along the angle of the beak, leaving the rounded curves open as marked on your pattern. Turn the beak so the right sides are facing out, loosely stuff the inside with fiberfill and hand sew it in place, centered in the middle of the face.

6 Select the type of eyes you would like from the Basics section (page 14). Attach the eyes above the beak.

7 Cut four Wing pieces from your black fleece using the template. Place two pieces right sides together and sew along the wing as marked on the pattern, leaving the straight edge open. Flip the wing so the right sides are facing out and sew along the edge of the wing to give it detail. Repeat this step to create the second wing. Hand sew both wings in place horizontally just above the brim, with one edge of each wing butted up to the face piece.

8 Refer to the Earflaps, Braids, and Tassels instructions in the Basics section (page 12) to make the "legs" of your penguin. Make the earflaps out of black fleece and the tassels out of yellow fleece.

9 Cut four Foot pieces from yellow fleece using the template. Place two of the pieces with right sides together and sew around the edge, leaving a 1-inch (2.5 cm) opening as marked on your pattern. Repeat for the second foot.

10 Place the end of your tassel braid into the opening of the foot and machine sew across it to secure. Repeat this step for the second foot.

enlarge all pieces by 200%

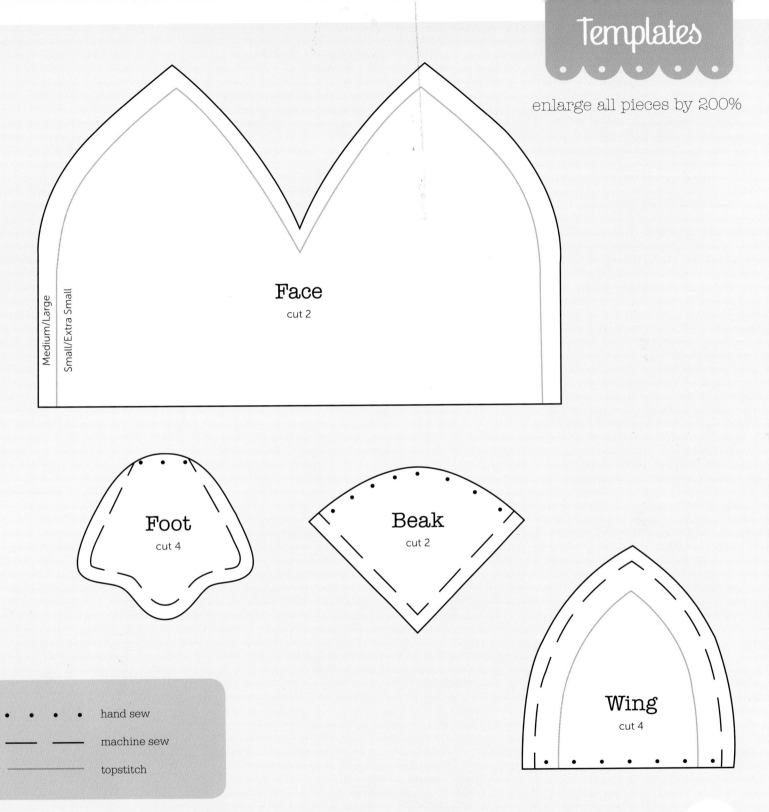

Medium/Large

Small/Extra Small

Face

cut 2

Foot

cut 4

Beak

cut 2

Wing

cut 4

• • • • •   hand sew

— — —   machine sew

————   topstitch

That's Some Pig

You'll be the pride of the sty with this little guy.

Tools and Materials

- Basic Sewing Tool Kit (page 9)
- ½ yard (45.7 cm) of pink fleece
- 1 pipe cleaner
- Black embroidery floss
- Polyester fiberfill
- Black beads, fleece, polyester fiberfill for eyes

{ If you're using 9 x 12-inch (22.9 x 30.5 cm) sheets of fleece, you will need 9 sheets of pink fleece. }

Instructions

1 Using the instructions and templates for the Basic Hat (page 10), create your hat using pink fleece.

2 To make the tail, cut a ⅝-inch-wide (1.6 cm) piece of pink fleece the length of your pipe cleaner. Wrap it around your pipe cleaner and ladder stitch along all edges.

3 Tuck ½ inch (1.3 cm) of the tail under the brim on the back of the hat. Pin and topstitch ¼ inch (6 mm) down from the top edge of the brim, making sure the tucked part of the tail is sewn into this seam. Bend the tail around your finger to create a spiral.

4 Cut one Side of Snout and one Front of Snout piece from pink fleece using the templates. Fold the Side of Snout in half with right sides together and sew along the short ends as indicated on the pattern. With wrong sides facing out, pin and sew the edge of the Front of Snout circle to an edge of the Side of Snout piece. Turn the right sides out and embroider the pig's nostrils with a full string of black embroidery floss and using the template markings as a guide. Stuff the snout and hand sew it on the hat, overlapping the edge of the brim.

5 Select the type of eyes you would like from the Basics section (page 14). Attach the eyes directly above the snout.

6 Cut four Ear pieces from pink fleece using the template. Place two pieces with the right sides together and sew along the curves of the ear as marked on your pattern, leaving the straight edge open. Turn the ear right side out and sew along the curves once again, topstitching ¼ inch (6 mm) from the outer edge. Repeat this step to make the second ear.

7 You will find that your ears will naturally turn toward one direction, which helps when deciding which side is

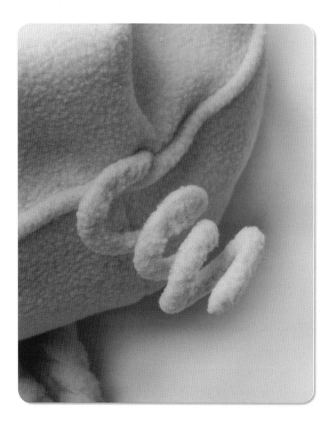

the front. The points should face forward. Place the ears about ½ inch (1.3 cm) above the eyeballs and ½ inch (1.3 cm) off the center seam that runs between the eyes. Hand sew them in place.

Tip: To help your ears stand up straight, sew the front of the ear on first. As you sew around to the back side of the ear, slightly pull the back layer toward the back of the hat. This creates a tripod for balance.

8 Refer to the Earflaps, Braids, and Tassels instructions in the Basics section (page 12) to add this feature. Make both the earflaps and tassels out of pink fleece.

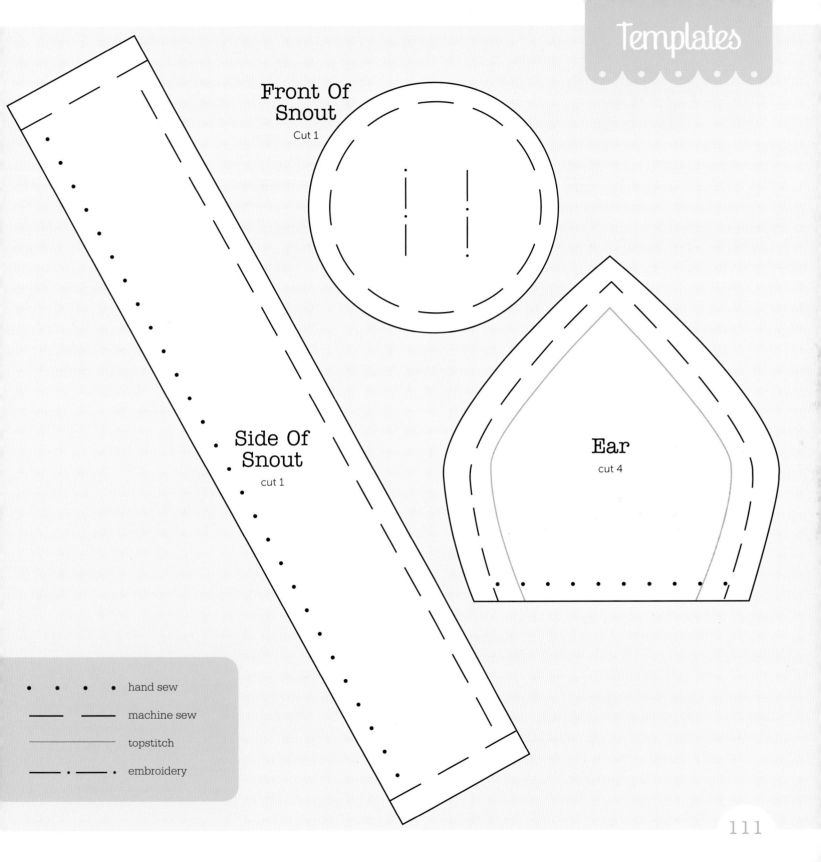

Front Of
Snout

Cut 1

Side Of
Snout

cut 1

Ear

cut 4

· · · · hand sew

— — — machine sew

———— topstitch

—·—·— embroidery

Peppy Puppy

This furry friend will warm you inside and out all winter long.

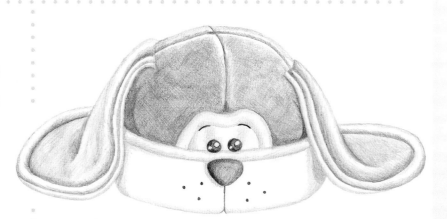

Tools and Materials

- Basic Sewing Tool Kit (page 9)
- ¼ yard (22.9 cm) of dark brown fleece
- ¼ yard (22.9 cm) of light brown fleece
- Scrap of black fleece
- Polyester fiberfill
- Black beads for eyes
- Black embroidery floss

{ If you're using 9 x 12-inch (22.9 x 30.5 cm) sheets of fleece, you will need 4 sheets of dark brown fleece, 4 sheets of light brown fleece, and 1 sheet or scrap of black fleece. }

Instructions

1 Using the instructions and templates for the Basic Hat (page 10), create your hat using dark brown fleece for the top part of your hat and light brown fleece for the brim. Find the seam on the brim of the hat and use this as the *philtrum*, or the natural groove that comes down from a dog's nose.

2 Cut two Face pieces from light brown fleece using the template. With right sides together, sew along the curve as marked on the template, leaving the straight edge open. Turn your piece so the right sides are facing out and sew along the curve once again, topstitching ⅝ inch (1.6 cm) from the outer edge. Tuck the bottom ½ inch (1.3 cm) of the Face piece under the brim, pin, and topstitch ¼ inch (6 mm) down from the top edge of the brim. Stitch once again along the topstitching on the Face piece securing it to the hat.

3 Cut two Ear pieces from dark brown fleece and two Ear pieces from light brown fleece using the templates. Place one of each color with right sides together and sew along the curved edge as marked on the template, leaving the straight edge open. Turn the ear right side out and guide your finger along the inside of the seam to help reduce any waviness. Topstitch ⅝ inch (1.6 cm) in from the curved edge, once again following the markings on the pattern. Repeat this step for the second ear.

4 Pin the ears about 2½ inches (6.4 cm) down from the center seam that runs from the front of the hat to the back and center them on the side seams. Sew them in place.

5 Cut one Nose piece out of black fleece using the template. Baste stitch around the outer edge and pull the thread to create a pouch. Stuff a small amount of fiberfill in this pouch, cinch it shut, and stitch the opening closed. Attach the nose just below the seam that goes around the brim of your hat.

6 Select the type of eyes you would like from the Basics section (page 14). Attach the eyes just above the brim, centered on the face piece.

7 Thread a needle with a full strand of embroidery floss and embroider along the philtrum and above the eyes (for eyebrows). Also, make three French knots on either cheek of the puppy if you desire.

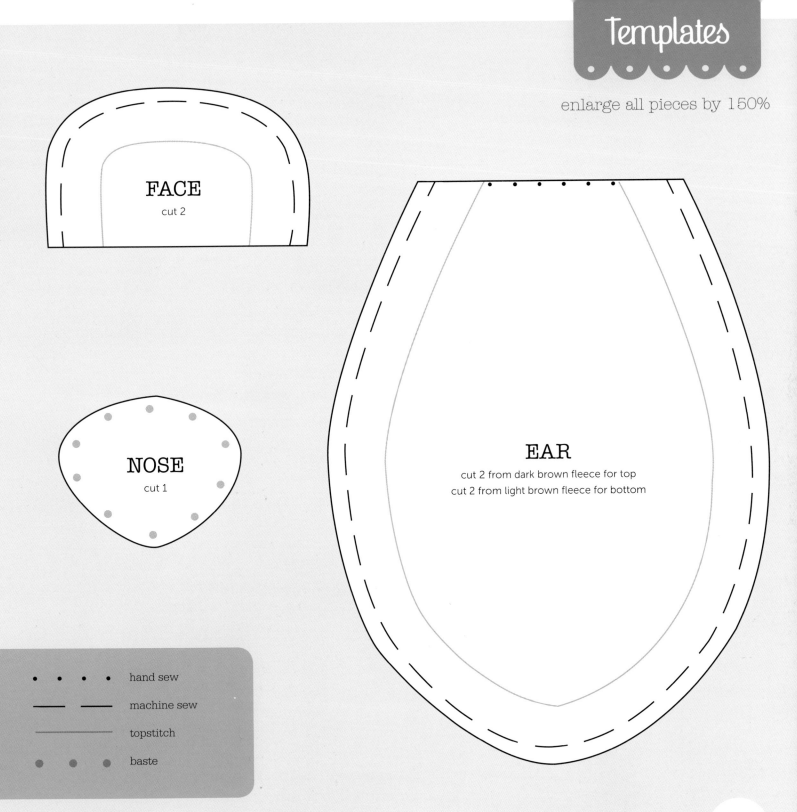

enlarge all pieces by 150%

FACE

cut 2

NOSE

cut 1

EAR

cut 2 from dark brown fleece for top
cut 2 from light brown fleece for bottom

· · · · hand sew

— — — machine sew

——— topstitch

● ● ● baste

Floppy-Eared Rabbit

Big ears make this one tons of fun to make and wear.

Tools and Materials

- Basic Sewing Tool Kit (page 9)
- ½ yard (45.7 cm) of white fleece
- ¼ yard (22.9 cm) of pink fleece
- Black beads for eyes
- Polyester fiberfill
- Black embroidery floss
- Black fishing line

{ If you're using 9 x 12-inch (22.9 x 30.5 cm) sheets of fleece, you will need 9 sheets of white fleece and 2 sheets of pink fleece. }

Instructions

1 Using the instructions and templates for the Basic Hat (page 10), create your hat using white fleece.

2 Sew a seam ¼ inch (6 mm) down from the top edge of the brim to secure it in place. Use the vertical seam on the brim of your hat to create the natural groove that comes down from a rabbit nose to the lips.

3 Cut two Ear pieces out of white fleece and two Ear pieces out of pink fleece using the template. Place one of each color with right sides together and sew along the two curved edges of the ear as marked on your pattern, leaving the straight edge open. Flip the ear right side out and guide your finger along the inside of the seam to help reduce the waviness. Topstitch ⅝ inch (1.6 cm) from the curved edges, once again following the markings on the pattern. Repeat this step for the second ear.

4 Fold the unfinished edge of the ear in half so the pink side is inside the fold. Baste stitch the unfinished edge together and pin the ears on either side of the hat with the pink on the underside. Feel free to take liberties with the positioning of the ears; hand sew them in place.

5 Select the type of eyes you would like from the Basics section (page 14). Attach the eyes just above the brim on the front of the hat.

6 Cut one Nose piece from pink fleece using the template. Baste stitch around the outer edge of this oval and pull the thread to create a pouch. Stuff a small amount of fiberfill in this pouch, cinch it shut, and sew the opening closed. Attach the nose near the top of the philtrum, or vertical seam, but below the seam going around the top of the brim.

7 Cut one Tail piece out of white fleece using the template. Using scissors or a rotary cutter, grid, and mat,

cut along the markings on the pattern leaving the ½-inch (1.3 cm) section in the middle uncut. Starting at one short side, roll the strip like a sleeping bag and secure it by sewing through the center of the roll. Next, tightly wrap thread around the roll three times and bring your needle through the center once again. Secure the pom-pom you just made with a knot and sew it to the back of the hat. Fluff the tail and trim pieces as necessary.

8 Embroider along the philtrum using three strands of black embroidery floss.

9 Thread your needle with black fishing line and insert it on one side of the nose and exit out the other side. Knot the whiskers close to the nose to keep them in place. Repeat twice more to make two sets of three whiskers. Trim them to the desired length, about 3 to 4 inches (7.6 to 10.2 cm).

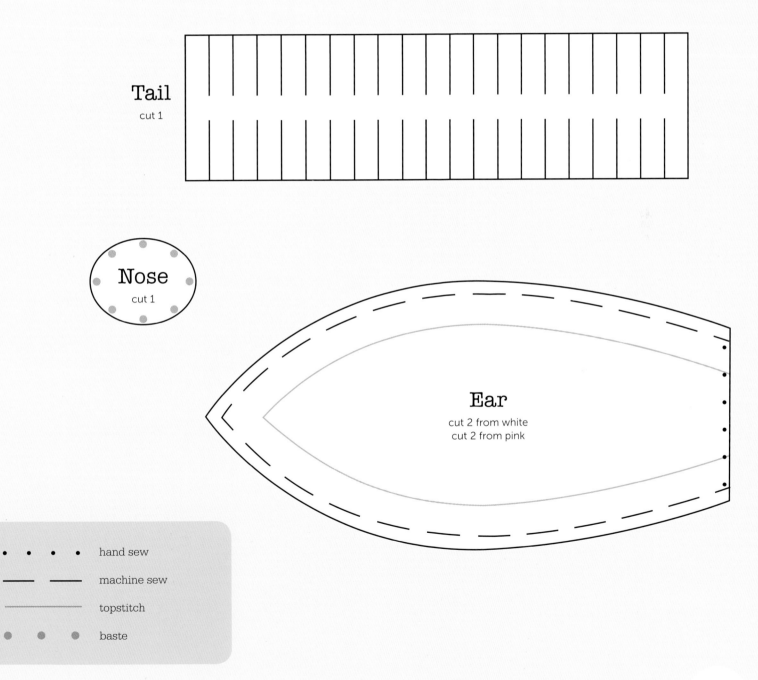

Tail
cut 1

Nose
cut 1

Ear
cut 2 from white
cut 2 from pink

· · · · hand sew

——— — machine sew

——— topstitch

● ● ● baste

Ruler of the Roost

A hat made for whoever wakes you up every morning.

Tools and Materials

- Basic Sewing Tool Kit (page 9)
- ¼ yard (45.7 cm) of off-white fleece
- ¼ yard (22.9 cm) of red fleece
- ⅛ yard (11.4 cm) of yellow fleece
- Polyester fiberfill
- Black beads, fleece, polyester fiberfill for eyes

{ If you're using 9 x 12-inch (22.9 x 30.5 cm) sheets of fleece, you will need 8 sheets of off-white fleece, 3 sheets of red fleece, and 2 sheets of yellow fleece. }

Instructions

1 Using the instructions and templates for the Basic Hat (page 10), create your hat using off-white fleece.

2 Topstitch ¼ inch (6 mm) down from the top edge of the brim to secure it in place.

3 Cut two Comb pieces from red fleece using the template, one with the pattern facing up and one with the pattern facing down. Place the two pieces with right sides together and machine sew along the wavy edge of the comb as marked on the pattern, leaving the bottom edge open. Turn the comb right side out and topstitch ¼ inch (6 mm) from the edge with your machine as marked on the pattern. Loosely stuff the comb with fiberfill and hand stitch the opening on the comb shut. Pin the back of the comb just above the brim and sew it in place along the seam going to the front of the hat.

4 Cut two Beak pieces from yellow fleece using the template. Place the two pieces with right sides together and machine sew along the edge of the beak as marked on your pattern, leaving the straight edge open. Turn the beak right side out and loosely stuff it with fiberfill. Hand stitch the beak onto the center front of the hat just above the brim.

5 Cut two Wattle 1 and two Wattle 2 pieces from red fleece using the template, cutting one piece of each pair with the pattern facing up and one piece with the pattern facing down. Place one pair with right sides together and sew around the edge of the wattle as marked on your pattern, leaving the straight edge open. Turn the wattle right side out and topstitch ¼ inch (6 mm) from the edge with your machine as marked on the pattern. Repeat this step for the second wattle. Hand sew the wattles together on the straight edges and hand sew them to the hat directly under the beak.

6 Select the type of eyes you would like from the Basics section (page 14), and sew the eyes in place directly above the beak.

7 Refer to the Earflaps, Braids, and Tassels instructions in the Basics section (page 12) to make the "legs" of your rooster. Use off-white fleece for the earflaps and yellow fleece for the braids and tassels.

enlarge all pieces by 125%

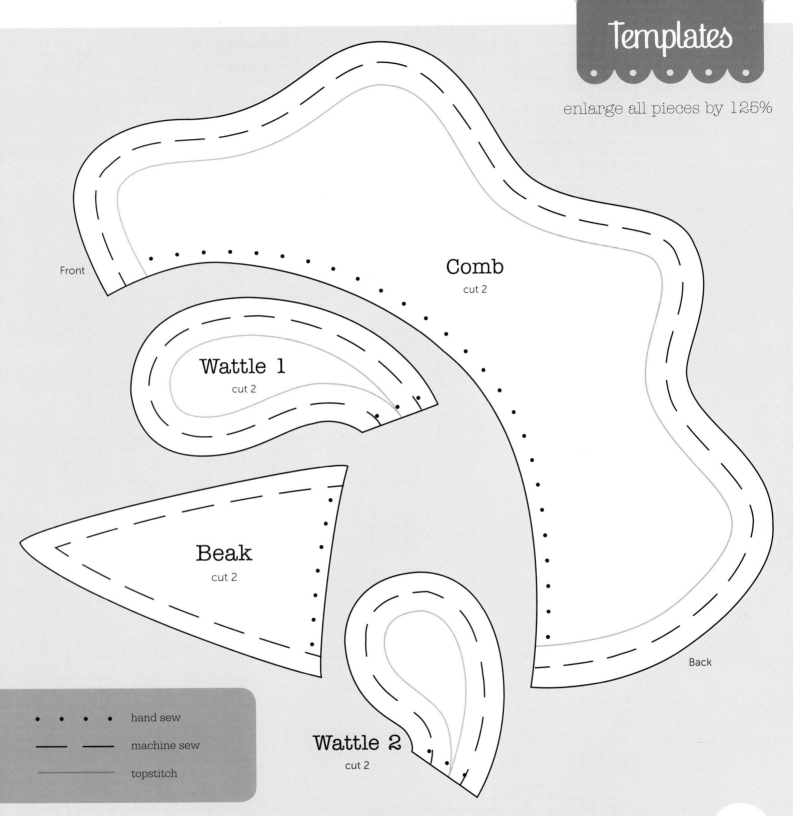

Front

Comb
cut 2

Wattle 1
cut 2

Beak
cut 2

Back

Wattle 2
cut 2

• • • •   hand sew

— — —   machine sew

———   topstitch

Spinning Spider

This design makes a great companion to the Feeling Batty hat (page 20).

Tools and Materials

- Basic Sewing Tool Kit (page 9)
- ¼ yard (22.9 cm) of purple fleece
- ¼ yard (22.9 cm) of black fleece
- Polyester fiberfill
- 8 flexible drinking straws, approximately ⁵⁄₁₆ inch (8 mm) in diameter
- Knitting needle (optional), US size 8 (5 mm) or smaller
- Black beads, fleece, polyester fiberfill for eyes

{ If you're using 9 x 12-inch (22.9 x 30.5 cm) sheets of fleece, you will need 6 sheets of purple fleece and 2 sheets of black fleece. }

Instructions

1 Using the instructions and templates for the Basic Hat (page 10), create your hat using purple fleece.

2 Topstitch ¼ inch (6 mm) down from the top edge of the brim to secure it in place.

3 Cut one Body piece from black fleece using the template. Knot one end of your thread and baste stitch around the outside of the circle. Pull the thread so your fleece forms a pouch and stuff it with fiberfill until the pouch is very full. Cinch the pouch together and sew the opening securely shut.

4 Cut eight Leg pieces from your black fleece using the template. If you are making an Extra-Small or Small hat, trim your straws to be 7 inches (17.8 cm) when fully extended. If you are making a Medium or Large hat, leave your straws at full length—which should be approximately 8¼ inches (21 cm) when fully extended. If you would like the legs to be very sturdy, gently stuff fiberfill into the straws using a US size 8 (5 mm) knitting needle as a tool.

5 Wrap a fleece Leg piece around a straw so the point is at the end of the straw's long section. Start ladder stitching at the point and continue up the side to the end of the short section of the straw. After all eight legs have been wrapped, stitch the end of each short section of the straw to the body. Attach four on one side of the spider and four on the other. Leave enough room on the front of your spider for eyes.

6 The decision is yours as to what eyes you would like on this crawly critter. You can choose to be realistic and sew on eight beads for eyes. If that gives you the heebie-jeebies, have your spider look friendly by making the Mini Surprised Eyes (page 14).

7 Take creative liberty for the placement of both your spider body and legs on the hat. Sew your spider sitting on top with its legs resting on the brim, or have it crawling on by sewing it on off-center.

enlarge all pieces by 125%

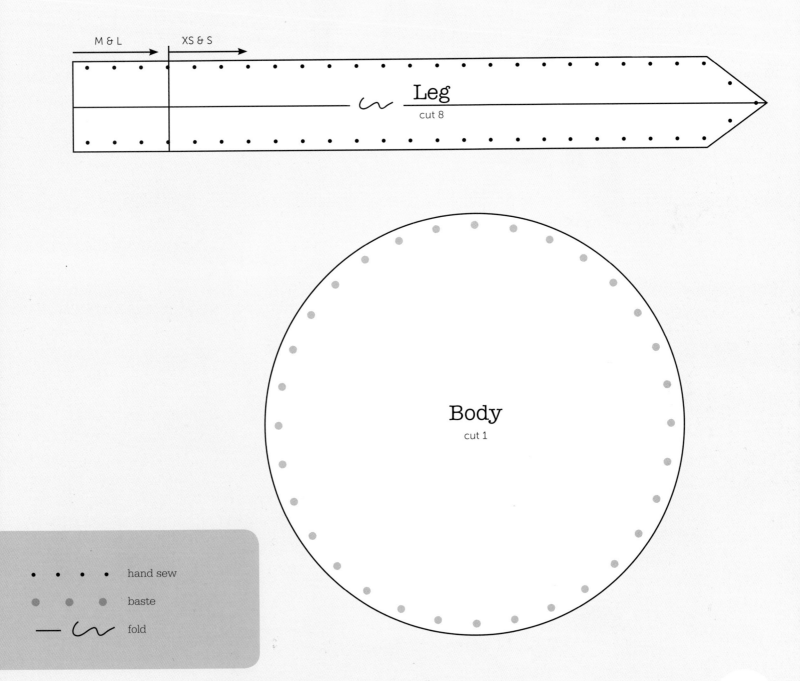

M & L

XS & S

Leg
cut 8

Body
cut 1

· · · · · hand sew

● ● ● baste

— ∿ fold

Tame Tiger

The bright orange fleece makes this an eye-catching design.

Tools and Materials

- Basic Sewing Tool Kit (page 9)
- ¼ yard (22.9 cm) of tie-dyed orange fleece
- ¼ yard (22.9 cm) of off-white fleece
- Scrap of solid orange fleece
- Scrap of pink fleece
- ⅛ yard (11.4 cm) of black fleece
- Black beads, fleece, polyester fiberfill for eyes
- Black fishing line

{ If you're using 9 x 12-inch (22.9 x 30.5 cm) sheets of fleece, you will need 2 sheets of tie-dyed orange fleece, 5 sheets of off-white fleece, 1 sheet or scrap of solid orange fleece, 1 sheet or scrap of pink fleece, and 1 sheet of black fleece. }

Instructions

1 Using the instructions and templates for the Basic Hat (page 10), create your hat using tie-dyed orange fleece for the top and off-white fleece for the brim.

2 Topstitch ¼ inch (6 mm) down from the top edge of the brim to secure it in place.

3 Cut one Top of Nose piece from solid orange fleece and one Bottom of Nose piece from pink fleece using the templates. Place the Top of Nose piece just above the brim, centered above the brim's vertical seam, and hand sew it in place using a ladder stitch. Line up the pink Bottom of Nose piece so the top corners match up with the bottom corners of the triangle. Hand sew the nose on the brim in this spot, again using a ladder stitch.

4 Cut two Ear pieces out of black fleece and two Ear pieces out of off-white fleece using the template. Place one of each color with right sides together and sew along the curved edge of the ear, leaving the straight edge open as marked on your pattern.

Repeat this step for the second ear. Flip the ears right side out and pin them on either side of the hat with the off-white sides facing forward 1½ inches (3.8 cm) off the center seam. Sew them in place, curving the ears shown at right.

5 Select the type of eyes you would like from the Basics section (page 14). Attach the eyes just above the brim on the front of the hat.

6 Cut one Stripe A piece, three Stripe B pieces, four Stripe C pieces, and four Stripe D pieces from black fleece using the templates. Using a ladder stitch, sew them on the hat according to **figure 1**.

7 Using black fishing line and your needle, make a knot at the end of the line. At the desired location for a whisker, insert the needle from the inside of the hat and come out the front. Make a knot close to the fleece to keep the whisker in place, and trim the whisker to the preferred length. Repeat so that you have three whiskers on each cheek.

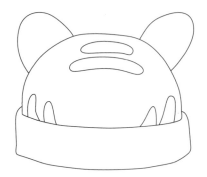

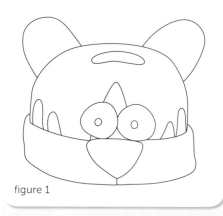

figure 1

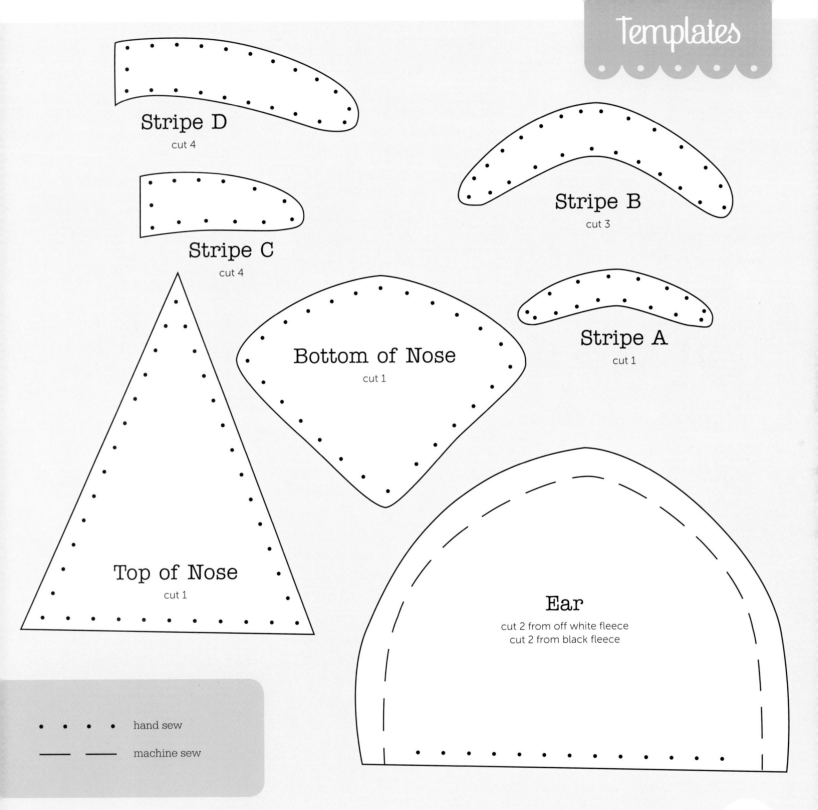

Stripe D
cut 4

Stripe C
cut 4

Stripe B
cut 3

Bottom of Nose
cut 1

Stripe A
cut 1

Top of Nose
cut 1

Ear
cut 2 from off white fleece
cut 2 from black fleece

• • • • • hand sew

——— machine sew

About the Author

Mary Rasch resides in northern Minnesota near the shore of Lake Superior. She is always passionate about the creative process, whether she is sewing, knitting, painting, drawing, or shooting photos. Mary frequently teaches classes, sells her creations at a local gift shop and online, and shares craft ideas through her blog, Mary's Makings (ilovemarysmakings.blogspot.com). Her work has been featured in publications such as *Stash Happy: Felt* (Lark Crafts). Although passionate about crafting, she is equally passionate about her family. She is married to a very supportive, fun-loving man and has a beautiful son and daughter who bless her life with humor, chaos, love, and fulfillment.

Models

Thanks to Gwendolyn Alvarado, Marley Curtis, Isabella Hanna, Sophia Hanna, Faith Medina, Sayil Pino, Boris Svrakov, and Tiffany Yoshida.

Index

B

Basic Hat Instructions 10
Basic Hat Templates 16
Basic Sewing Tool Kit 9
Beads 8

E

Ear and Eye Templates 19
Earflaps, Braids, and Tassels 12
Eye Instructions 14

F

Fiberfill 9
Fleece 6

I

Interfacing 9

L

Lining 13

P

Pins 7
Projects . . . See Table of Contents

S

Seams 11
Sewing Needle 7

T

Thread 7
Tools and Materials 6
Tracing paper 9